#1 *NEW YORK TIMES* BESTSELLING AUTHOR

MIKE EVANS

JEW-HATRED

AND THE

CHURCH

TIMEWORTHY
BOOKS

P.O. BOX 30000, PHOENIX, AZ 85046

Published by TimeWorthy Books
P. O. Box 30000
Phoenix, AZ 85046

Design: Peter Gloege | LOOK Design Studio

Hardcover: 978-1-62961-131-0
Paperback: 978-1-62961-132-7
    Canada: 978-1-62961-133-4

This book is lovingly dedicated to
Dr. Jack Hayford,
a man who casts a giant shadow in the
church world today. He has served as senior pastor
of The Church On The Way in Van Nuys, CA, as well
as founding King's College and Seminary where
pastors are trained. He also served as president of the
International Church of the Foursquare Gospel.

Pastor Hayford is a creative genius,
authoring numerous books as well as writing songs.
Perhaps his most well-known musical creation is
"Majesty," one of the top 100 hymns of modern times.
It is my distinct honor to call him my friend.

FOREWORD 7

1 | BEGINNING AT THE BEGINNING 11

2 | ACTS OF THE EARLY CHURCH 27

3 | THE GROWTH OF THE EARLY CHURCH 47

4 | CRUEL & COLD-BLOODED CUSTODIANS OF ROME 65

5 | FLAVIUS VALERIUS CONSTANTINUS, EMPEROR 79

6 | APOSTASY ARISES 101

7 | CONSTANTINE CHANGES CHURCH CUSTOMS 117

8 | ANTI-SEMITISM PROLIFERATES 129

9 | MURDER AND MAYHEM 145

10 | TRIALS AND TERRORS 155

11 | THE POGROMS OF 1391 165

12 | DIVISIVE DISUNITY 175

13 | THE SPANISH INQUISITION: SUFFERING INFLICTED 185

14 | TOMÁS DE TORQUEMADA, INQUISITOR GENERAL 193

15 | MISERY, MAYHEM, AND MURDER 203

16 | THOSE WHO GO DOWN TO THE SEA IN SHIPS... 217

17 | ROME AND REFORMATION 235

18 | ANIMOSITY BEGETS ANTI-SEMITISM 251

19 | HITLER'S "JUSTIFICATION" 265

20 | ANTI-SEMITISM: ALIVE AND GROWING 279

21 | RECONCILIATION OR CHANGE 291

ENDNOTES 307

AUTHOR BIO 319

FOREWORD

MORE THAN two thousand years ago, the early church was born from the rancorous division between Jews in Palestine and Jewish converts to Christianity. It was spurred by the birth, death, and resurrection of Jesus of Nazareth. The church grew out of the vicious persecution heaped upon its adherents, and the gospel was spread by Christians who fled Jerusalem and its environs seeking a safe harbor to weather the storm of hostility. It was a cyclone that threatened to destroy the battered believers.

What caused the acrimony between the two groups? Was it jealousy? Fear? Politics? Perhaps it was a bit of all those motivations, but ultimately the political climate played a massive role in the roots of anti-Semitism that erupted throughout Europe following the conversion of Constantine in AD 312.

Jesus of Nazareth was born into a culture of foreign occupation and political dominance by the Roman legions. He was not insulated from having to deal with the soldiers who strode throughout the land, sometimes trampling everything—and everyone—in their path.

In Matthew 22, Jesus was challenged by the Pharisees and Herodians (a political party whose members supported Herod). Jesus was asked,

> "Is it lawful to pay taxes to Caesar, or not?" But Jesus perceived their wickedness, and said, "Why do you test Me, you hypocrites? Show Me the tax money." So they brought Him a denarius. And He said to them, "Whose image and inscription *is* this?" They said to Him, "Caesar's." And He said to them, "Render therefore to Caesar the things that are Caesar's, and to God the things that are God's." (Matthew 22:17–21 NKJV)

Professor Lance Pape of Brite Divinity School, Texas Christian University in Fort Worth, Texas, wrote:

> Whatever we render unto Caesar, or to the retirement fund, or to the offering basket at church, we can never afford to forget this: we belong entirely to God. We may divide our budget, but we must never divide our

allegiance. The coin of our realm bears the image of dead presidents, but each of us bears another. Our Emperor said: "Let us make humankind in our image, according to our likeness." We must never forget to render unto God the things that are God's.[1]

In supporting blatant anti-Semitism, what many seem to forget is that Jesus was Jewish. Neither He nor His disciples were hostile to Judaism. He kept the law and attended the appointed feasts. What transpired, then, to place our Lord firmly on the opposite side of the line drawn between Him and the Pharisees, Sadducees, and Herodians? The answer lies in political expediency. The Pharisees had orchestrated a tense peace arrangement between the Jews and the authorities in Rome. The high priest had built a wall around himself and his followers—one that allowed him to enjoy the prestige afforded his position.

Suddenly, a thirty-year-old Galilean, one who affirmed that He was indeed the Messiah, began to chip away at the wall. It created abject fear among the Sanhedrin; it threatened their safe haven and, perhaps just as importantly, their income. As the number of Jesus' followers increased, so did the anxiety in the hearts of the Jewish leaders. Frightened at the thought of another onslaught by the Romans, the Pharisees determined that the only resolution was to kill Jesus of Nazareth and scatter His disciples. That scurrilous decision, the move that would save them from further interference from Rome, brings us to the truth behind the words of Caiaphas in John 11:50 (NLT):

> You don't realize that it's better for you
> that one man should die for the people than
> for the whole nation to be destroyed.

What transpired was a family feud based on the differences between Old Testament law and New Testament grace. It came to culmination following the conversion of Constantine as Christianity was influenced by the Roman desire to disentangle itself from the crucifixion of Jesus. The result was the unmitigated lie that the Jews had crucified Him. It is a falsehood that has raced from one end of the earth to the other, igniting pogroms, slaughters, persecutions, and finally its ultimate manifestation—the Holocaust that cost the lives of six million innocent Jewish men, women, and children.

We will explore in the pages of this book how the early church wandered so far from its purpose: "to seek and to save the lost" (Luke 19:10 ESV).

BEGINNING AT THE BEGINNING

THE CHURCH of Jesus Christ began with one Man who first chose twelve men, and then later commissioned seventy others to go forth in ministry. After His ascension, the group gathered in the upper room. There, approximately 120 men and women were baptized in the Holy Spirit and received boldness and power to go forth and preach the good news of salvation through the blood of Jesus, the sacrificial Lamb of God.

The book of Acts is the historical account of the disciples who selflessly and sacrificially spread the gospel from Jerusalem to Judea and Samaria, and then to the ends of the earth. It is the dynamic and vibrant link between the narratives of Matthew, Mark, Luke, and John, to the epistles that follow. While the book is entitled "Acts of the Apostles," it could more accurately be labeled "The Acts of Jesus as He worked through His followers by the Holy Spirit."

It is widely accepted that Luke, a Gentile physician and writer of the book that bears his name, also authored this book. According to Bible History Online:

> Scholars agree that Acts was written around 62 or 63 AD. It is interesting to note that Luke never intimated the event of the destruction of the Temple and Jerusalem in 70 AD within the book of Acts. Jerusalem is pictured as a currently thriving center of Judaism, with the temple service and sacrifices being carried out in a normal manner. After 70 AD everything changed and it would have been obvious if Luke had written Acts after 70 AD. Luke concludes Acts with Paul in Rome living in a hired house, and awaiting trial before Caesar (Acts 28:30). This would have been 61 or 62 AD obviously before the great persecution of Christians by Nero and the destruction of Jerusalem in 70 AD.[2]

Many also agree that Luke and Acts were meant to be

a two-volume endeavor, as the first verse of Acts closely links it to Luke:

> I wrote the first narrative, Theophi-lus, about all that Jesus began to do and teach until the day He was taken up, after He had given orders through the Holy Spirit to the apostles He had chosen. (Acts 1:1–2 HCSB)

Some scholars surmise that Theophilus may have been an official of Rome with whom Luke wished to establish a credible foundation for his faith in Jesus Christ. Together, these two books of the New Testament written by Mark encompass about 30 percent of the biblical chronicle—more than that written by Paul.[3] Acts is an eyewitness account of men and the might of the Holy Spirit working in and through them. Although Jesus had ascended into heaven, there was still work to be done—and He commissioned a group to carry on His mission. Those men faced unparalleled opposition while performing miracles and delivering—upon threat of death—the most important message the world would ever hear. Many of them did indeed die while assuming the task that God had called and anointed them to do.

Scottish Bible scholar and theologian Alexander MacLaren provided great insight into Luke's text:

It is the unfinished record of an incomplete work. The theme is the work of Christ through the ages, of which each successive depository of His energies can do but a small portion, and must leave that portion unfinished; the book does not so much end as stop. It is a fragment, because the work of which it tells is not yet a whole.

If, then, we put these two things—the beginning and the ending of the Acts—together, I think we get some thoughts about what Christ began to do and teach on earth; what He continues to do and teach in heaven; and how small and fragmentary a share in that work each individual servant of His has. . . . The book must be incomplete, because the work of which it is the record does not end until 'He shall have delivered up the Kingdom to the Father, and God shall be all in all.' So the work of each man is but a fragment of that great work. Every man inherits unfinished tasks from his predecessors, and leaves unfinished tasks to his successors.[4]

The one thread that links the first verse of Acts chapter one inexorably with the final verse in chapter twenty-eight is the resurrection of Jesus Christ and forgiveness of sin offered through His name alone. Perhaps in writing Acts, Luke was intent on convincing the multitudes of the authenticity of the ministry of the Messiah. Throughout the book, the apostles were used by the Holy Spirit to perform signs, wonders, and miracles during the time of transition from a ministry centered in Jerusalem to one with worldwide outreach. John Stott in his book *The Message of Acts* reveals how important was the preaching of God's Word through the sermons recorded in that text:

> No fewer than nineteen significant Christian speeches occur in his second volume . . . there are eight by Peter (in chapters 1, 2, 3, 4, 5, 10, 11 and 15) . . . one each by Stephen and James . . . and nine by Paul (five sermons in chapters 13, 14, 17, 20, and 28, and four defense speeches in chapters 22 to 26). Approximately 20% of Luke's text is devoted to addresses by Peter and Paul; if Stephen's speech is added, the percentage rises to about 25%.[5]

What exactly, according to Acts 1:1–2, was the church

called to do? The work of Christ's disciples was to be one of spreading the good news—the story of the birth, death, and resurrection of Jesus. The apostles were to take up the cross of Christ and engage in the pursuit of seeking and reconciling lost men and women to God the Father. Its message was, and still is, that of John 1:1, 14 (NKJV):

> In the beginning was the Word, and the Word was with God, and the Word was God. . . . And the Word became flesh and dwelt among us, and we beheld His glory, the glory as of the only begotten of the Father, full of grace and truth.

Before His departure, Jesus sat down with His disciples and imparted to them what has come to be known as the Great Commission:

> Then Jesus came to them and said, "All authority in heaven and on earth has been given to me. Therefore go and make disciples of all nations, baptizing them in the name of the Father and of the Son and of the Holy Spirit, and teaching them to obey everything I have commanded you. And surely I am with

you always, to the very end of the age." (Matthew 28:18–20 NIV)

A walk through the book of Acts leaves the reader with the distinct impression that the disciples were determined to accept the charge given them. They were not walking the streets of Jerusalem, traversing dusty roads of Judea, or sailing the wide and dangerous seas of their own volition; they had a higher calling, a definite plan and purpose they were determined to fulfill. They were tools in the hands of God, employed to build His church.

Rather than write a biography on each of the twelve disciples, Luke included little about each of the inner circle. He could certainly have written at length about the lives of Peter, James, Paul, and John. He chose instead not to focus on the instrument but rather on the Master Builder. Peter fades from view in chapter 15; James upon his martyrdom in chapter 12. John finds a voice only in the first four chapters; Barnabas also drops from the narrative in chapter 15. Even Paul, the intrepid apostle, finds himself imprisoned in Rome in the final chapter of Luke's missive. British evangelist, pastor, and Bible scholar G. Campbell Morgan commented on Acts:

When we come to the study of this book, therefore, we must understand that it is not merely a mechanical story of the journeying of Paul, or of the doings of Peter. It is intended to reveal to us the processes through which Christ proceeds in new power, consequent upon the things He began to do and teach, toward the ultimate and final victory, which we see symbolized in the mystic language of Revelation.[6]

Could it also be that Luke wanted readers in ages to come to know that the work of the church was accomplished by the hands of a group of men who fashioned their own doctrine? No, the gospel of Jesus Christ was carried forth by disciples who were hand-chosen to convey His message. They were not self-styled superstars with their own agendas and religious beliefs; they were the laborers sent forth into the harvest. They were eyewitnesses testifying to what they had experienced while walking the dusty Judean roads and hills with their Lord. They were the "called, chosen and faithful"[7] servants of the Sovereign God.

The ministry of those men—and women—was productive and prolific—3,000 on the day of Pentecost (Acts 2); Phillip's witness to the Ethiopian eunuch (Acts 8); Peter's ministry to Cornelius and his household (Acts 10); the conversion of Lydia and of the Philippian jailer (Acts 16). What produced this and many other conversion experiences in Acts? It was simply the obedience of dedicated men who responded to the urging of the Holy Spirit.

It was not, by any means, a calling devoid of suffering and harassment. Luke's account is as filled with tyranny as it is with transformation: Stephen was stoned; Peter and John were beaten and thrown into prison; James was killed with a sword; and later in his ministry, Paul was stoned, imprisoned, and beaten. It was a period fraught with danger and death. When Peter and John were released from prison to appear before the Sanhedrin, they vowed to continue to preach the good news of Jesus Christ. Gamaliel, the leading Jewish teacher of his day and an unlikely champion, gave the following advice to the council members who were determined to kill the two apostles:

> Men of Israel, take care what you are plan-
> ning to do to these men! Some time ago there
> was that fellow Theudas, who pretended to
> be someone great. About 400 others joined
> him, but he was killed, and all his followers

went their various ways. The whole movement came to nothing. After him, at the time
of the census, there was Judas of Galilee. He
got people to follow him, but he was killed,
too, and all his followers were scattered. So
my advice is, leave these men alone. Let them
go. If they are planning and doing these
things merely on their own, it will soon be
overthrown. But if it is from God, you will
not be able to overthrow them. You may even
find yourselves fighting against God! (Acts
5:35–39 NLT)

Saul must have been incredulous! His mentor was actually defending the very people he had set out to destroy. Saul
spewed forth threats; Gamaliel offered wisdom. Would the
Sanhedrin succumb to such quiet guidance, or would its
members stand and fight what Saul saw as a threat to the
very existence of the Jews? Fortunately for the disciples—and
eventually Saul himself—the group heeded Gamaliel's wise
words.

How did the men who faced imminent danger and martyrdom respond? Acts 5:41–42 reveals that the two disciples,
Peter and John, rejoiced "that they were counted worthy to

suffer shame for His name. And daily in the temple, and in every house, they did not cease teaching and preaching Jesus as the Christ" (NKJV). With painful furrows sliced into their backs, the two moved again into the trenches and began to preach the gospel of Jesus Christ to all who would listen.

The author of Hebrews provides additional insight into what those early believers endured:

> Some were laughed at and their backs cut open with whips, and others were chained in dungeons. Some died by stoning and some by being sawed in two; others were promised freedom, if they would renounce their faith, then were killed with the sword. Some went about in skins of sheep and goats, wandering over deserts and mountains, hiding in dens and caves. They were hungry and sick and ill-treated—too good for this world. (Hebrews 11:36–38 TLB)

Before the day of Pentecost, these same individuals were frightened, cowering behind walls and locked doors. After baptism in the Holy Spirit a new boldness transformed them, a newfound confidence sustained them, and a previously unknown urgency to preach the kingdom of God and of His

Christ to the known world drove them. God knit together a diverse band of men and women from every social stratum and from every ethnicity to accomplish His work on earth. The Holy Spirit enlisted Barnabas (a rabbi), Simeon, who was called Niger (thought to have been a black man from Niger), Lucius (a Greek from a colony in Libya), Manaen (a foster brother of Herod), and Paul (a Pharisee and persecutor of the church). What an eclectic band of brothers, but what amazing feats they accomplished!

Early in the book, Luke makes clear what the purpose of the early church was to be. In Acts 6:4, he wrote, "But we will give ourselves continually to prayer and to the ministry of the word" (NKJV). As a result, the church grew as the Word of God and the chronicle of the works of Jesus spread wherever the feet of those men touched the soil. Seeds were planted; lives were changed; "And the Lord added to the church daily those who were being saved" (Acts 2:47 NKJV).

The roots of today's church are firmly embedded in the history of the early church in the book of Acts. Eusebius, the chronicler of the history of the church, wrote of the apostles:

> Meanwhile the holy apostles and disciples
> of our Savior were scattered over the whole
> world. Thomas, tradition tells us, was chosen

for Parthia, Andrew for Scythia, John for Asia, where he remained till his death at Ephesus. Peter seems to have preached in Pontus, Galatia and Bithynia, Cappadocia and Asia, to the Jews of the Dispersion. (Cf. 1 Peter 1.1) Finally, he came to Rome where he was crucified, head downwards at his request. What need be said of Paul, who from Jerusalem as far as Illyricum preached in all the fullness the gospel of Christ (Romans 15:19), and later was martyred in Rome under Nero?[8]

Paul had written to the Ephesians that their faith was built upon the "foundation of the apostles and prophets, Jesus Christ Himself being the chief cornerstone" (Ephesians 2:20 NKJV). I'm reminded of the words of songwriter Edward Mote, who penned:

My hope is built on nothing less
Than Jesus' blood and righteousness.
I dare not trust the sweetest frame,
But wholly trust in Jesus' Name.[9]

When Luke laid down his stylus at the closing of his missive, he knew little of the deaths of those men who had so faithfully served the early church. According to John Foxe, author of *Foxe's Book of Martyrs*, the twelve men who followed Jesus suffered immeasurable pain before being reunited with their Lord. Tradition indicates that Matthew was killed by the sword in Ethiopia; James, the brother of Jesus, refused to deny his faith and was thrown down from a pinnacle of the temple; Bartholomew (Nathanael) was flayed with a whip while preaching in Armenia; Andrew was hung from a cross with ropes where he remained for two days before succumbing; Thomas, while ministering in India, was stabbed to death with a spear; Matthias (Judas' replacement) was stoned and then beheaded. The other apostles died equally horrific deaths, except for John: he was boiled in oil and then dumped on the Isle of Patmos. From that barren and isolated spot, he recovered and wrote the book of Revelation. After he was freed, John returned to the area now known as Turkey. He died there of old age—the *only* disciple to die of natural causes.

Each of the apostles could have said, as did Paul:

> I have fought the good fight, I have finished the race, I have kept the faith. Finally, there is laid up for me the crown of righteousness, which the Lord, the righteous Judge, will give

to me on that Day, and not to me only but also to all who have loved His appearing. (2 Timothy 4:7–8, NKJV)

ACTS OF THE EARLY CHURCH

THE NEW TESTAMENT book of Acts is fundamentally the history of the early church. Acts chapter two takes place on the day of Pentecost. In chapter one Jesus' disciples had stood atop the Mount of Olives and watched in awe as their Lord was taken up into the clouds. Before His ascension, Jesus had instructed His followers to return to Jerusalem, where they were to tarry until endued with the power of the Holy Spirit. After receiving the "promise of the Father" Peter stood and then preached to the crowds jamming the streets of Jerusalem for the Feast of Pentecost. Upon hearing the disciple's sermon, 3,000 believed and were saved. Other encounters recorded in the book of Acts include Philip teaching a group of Samaritans, followed by his visit with the Ethiopian eunuch in chapter eight. Perhaps one of the most significant encounters and one that greatly impacted the early church and the growth of Christianity was that of Saul of Tarsus with the risen Jesus on the road to Damascus, an event we will consider in depth in the following chapter. Saul would later become known as the apostle Paul, author of fourteen books of the New Testament: 1 and 2 Thessalonians, Galatians, 1 and 2 Corinthians, Romans, Hebrews, Ephesians, Philippians, Colossians, Philemon, 1 and 2 Timothy, and Titus.

Saul's one purpose in life was to halt the proliferation of the cult of Christians that had sprung up in Israel after the crucifixion of the rogue preacher, Jesus of Nazareth. The conversion of Jews to Christianity had to be stopped at all costs. Under the auspices of the chief priests, Saul launched a hunting expedition to Damascus and other foreign cities to round up and, under the threat of imprisonment and/or death, force as many of the fugitives as possible to blaspheme the name of Jesus Christ. Should the threats fail, the prisoners would be returned to Jerusalem to face the wrath of the Sanhedrin. It was with that purpose in mind that Saul of Tarsus gathered his entourage and chose one of the two available routes for the 150-mile trek northward, a trip that would have taken one to two weeks to complete.

As he took his first steps outside the city on the long, dusty road that led to Damascus, Saul had no idea what lay ahead and the momentous role he would have in history. One of the things we don't know about Saul is what elicited his hatred for and the cruelty with which he treated those who had chosen to follow Christ. The very mention of his name caused fear and trembling amidst those who had fled to surrounding countries. We first meet Saul in Acts 7 when he can be seen on the fringes of the outraged mob that stoned Stephen to death, one of the first deacons in the early church. Saul is guarding the belongings of the bloodthirsty throng:

> The Jewish leaders were stung to fury by Stephen's accusation and ground their teeth in rage. . . . Then they mobbed him, putting their hands over their ears, and drowning out his voice with their shouts, and dragged him out of the city to stone him. The official witnesses—the executioners—took off their coats and laid them at the feet of a young man named Paul. (Acts 7:54, 57–58 TLB)

Perhaps Saul of Tarsus had the blood of the righteous Stephen spattered on his dusty feet and along the hem of his own robe. His hands might have been clenched in rage, his face twisted with hatred for the young man who had been so brutally attacked. The only thing that infuriated Saul more than Stephen's sermon was the name of the One about which Stephen preached and for whom he had died.

Little is known of Saul's childhood, only that he was from Tarsus, a city in Cilicia. Author John Pollock provides some understanding into the life of the devout Jew:

> Paul's parents were Pharisees, members of the party most fervent in Jewish nationalism and strict in obedience to the Law of Moses. They sought to guard their offspring against contamination. Friendships with Gentile children were discouraged. Greek ideas were despised. Though Paul from infancy could speak Greek . . . and had a working knowledge of Latin, his family at home spoke Aramaic, the language of Judea, a derivative of Hebrew.
>
> They looked to Jerusalem as Islam looks to Mecca. Their privileges as freemen of Tarsus and Roman citizens were nothing to the high honor of being Israelites, the People

of Promise, to whom alone the Living God had revealed His glory and His plans . . . By his thirteenth birthday, Paul had mastered Jewish history, the poetry of the psalms, and the majestic literature of the prophets. . . . During the next five or six years, he sat at the feet of Gamaliel . . . Paul learned to dissect a text until scores of possible meanings were disclosed . . . to debate in question-and-answer style known in the ancient world as "diatribe," and to expound, for a rabbi was not only part preacher but part lawyer. . . . He had a powerful mind which could lead to a seat on the Sanhedrin.[10]

We do know that from the time he became a profitable lawyer in Jerusalem until his life-changing trip to Damascus, Saul's pursuit and persecution of believers was ruthless. After his conversion, he wrote in Galatians 1:13, "For you have heard of my former conduct in Judaism, how I persecuted the church of God beyond measure and tried to destroy it" (NKJV).

Acts 9:1–2 (NKJV) presents a picture of Saul's state of mind after the death of Stephen:

Then Saul, still breathing threats and murder against the disciples of the Lord, went to the high priest and asked letters from him to the synagogues of Damascus, so that if he found any who were of the Way, whether men or women, he might bring them bound to Jerusalem.

Why Damascus? Did the Sanhedrin really hold such sway in a city of Syria? According to *Clarke's Commentary on the Bible*:

In every country where there were Jews and synagogues, the power and authority of the Sanhedrin and high priest were acknowledged: just as papists in all countries acknowledge the authority of the pope. And as there can be but one pope, and one conclave, so there could be but one high priest, and one Sanhedrin; and this is the reason why the high priest and Sanhedrin at Jerusalem had authority over all Jews, even in the most distant countries.[11]

With papers in hand, Saul eagerly traversed mile after mile on his journey from Jerusalem to Damascus.

Hour after hour, anticipation built; there were heretics to unearth, apostates to apprehend, renegades to arrest—and Saul of Tarsus was the man for the job. His anger knew no bounds, his determination unchecked. In that day's version of a diplomatic pouch, the heretic hunter carried legal documents that gave him permission to arrest followers of the Way. In his comments on this chapter of Acts, John Calvin referred to Saul as "a cruel wolf" who was "not only turned into a sheep, but did also put on the nature of a shepherd."[12]

Late in the day, probably weary, perhaps thirsty, no doubt eager to complete his journey and his task, Saul neared the outskirts of the city. Suddenly he was stopped in his tracks by a light brighter than the noonday sun. Engulfed by the intensity of the radiance, Saul fell backward to the ground and hid his face. Saul might have considered the event a rogue lightning strike accompanied by a roll of thunder but would soon learn it was much more than happenstance. He was about to find that he was no longer in control of his life. Someone greater than he—the King of all creation—was about to make His presence known in the life of an avowed terrorist. Saul simply thought he was persecuting people in an attempt to stop the spread of a cult. In the twinkling of an eye, he learned that he was instead persecuting the Messiah of prophecy—the One foretold by the ancient prophets, priests, and kings.

From the midst of the glow, he heard a voice:

"Saul, Saul, why are you persecuting Me?" And he said, "Who are You, Lord?" Then the Lord said, "I am Jesus, whom you are persecuting. It is hard for you to kick against the goads." So he, trembling and astonished, said, "Lord, what do You want me to do?" Then the Lord said to him, "Arise and go into the city, and you will be told what you must do." And the men who journeyed with him stood speechless, hearing a voice but seeing no one. Then Saul arose from the ground, and when his eyes were opened he saw no one. But they led him by the hand and brought him into Damascus. (Acts 9:4–8 NKJV)

Saul might well have thought of the 139th psalm of David that asks the question:

Where can I go from Your Spirit? Or where can I flee from Your presence? (v. 7 NKJV)

He would soon learn the answer to David's query: Nowhere!

If I ascend into heaven, You are there; If I make my bed in hell, behold, You are there. (v. 8 NKJV)

Author and theologian Charles Swindoll explains the expression Christ used to challenge Saul:

> Apparently, "to kick against the goads" was a common expression found in both Greek and Latin literature—a rural image, which rose from the practice of farmers goading their oxen in the fields. Though unfamiliar to us, everyone in that day understood.
>
> Goads were typically made from slender pieces of timber, blunt on one end and pointed on the other. Farmers used the pointed end to urge a stubborn ox into motion. Occasionally, the beast would kick at the goad. The more the ox kicked, the more likely it would stab into the flesh of its leg, causing greater pain. Saul's conversion could appear to us as having been a sudden encounter with Christ. But based on the Lord's expression regarding him kicking back, I believe He'd been working on him for years, prodding and goading him.[13]

After taking shelter in the city, Saul, blinded by the

dazzling light and undoubtedly frightened by his encounter, spent three tortuous days, neither eating nor drinking, awaiting instructions from the One who had spoken to him. During those three days, Saul must have recounted the life-changing appointment on the road time and again. Surely he rehearsed everything he had ever seen or heard about Jesus of Nazareth and the people of the Way. It is possible Saul had even been a part of a group that had tried to confound Jesus. If so, he had even more to consider.

While Saul was contemplating his past, God was busily working on another man who would be sent to accomplish His will—Ananias. He, too, was about to be stopped in mid-stride by a vision. In Acts 9:11–16 (NKJV), we read of the encounter:

> So the Lord said to [Ananias], "Arise and go to the street called Straight, and inquire at the house of Judas for one called Saul of Tarsus, for behold, he is praying. And in a vision he has seen a man named Ananias coming in and putting his hand on him, so that he might receive his sight." Then Ananias answered, "Lord, I have heard from many about this man, how much harm he has done

to Your saints in Jerusalem. And here he has
authority from the chief priests to bind all
who call on Your name." But the Lord said to
him, "Go, for he is a chosen vessel of Mine to
bear My name before Gentiles, kings, and the
children of Israel. For I will show him how
many things he must suffer for My name's
sake."

Ananias might have responded, "WHAT? Saul of Tarsus?
Lord, don't you know this guy?" God did not equivocate
or vacillate; He simply said, "Go!" Ananias set out to find
Saul, who was cowering behind a locked door somewhere
in Damascus—sleepless, hungry, and afraid.

Finally, a knock was heard on the door of Saul's abode.
It was followed by the entry of Ananias. Conquering his
own fear and doubt, the one sent by God to minister to
Saul entered the room with what surely must have been
uncertain steps on trembling legs. Ananias, in an unsteady
voice, introduced himself to Saul. Certainly, after three
long and terrifying days, Saul was ready to hear all that
Ananias had to say. Girding himself with the power of the
Holy Spirit, God's messenger began to relay the edict he had
been sent to deliver. Saul would learn what the future held

for him—physical and emotional suffering, pain, deprivation, and more. Ananias could have disobeyed the heavenly vision and stayed home, wracked by fear. Saul could have made the decision to crawl back to Jerusalem, a broken man, a blind outcast who could no longer worship in the temple. Either option could have forever changed the trajectory of the early church. Ananias chose obedience, and Saul chose to commit his life to the Lord of Lords. After Ananias placed hands on Saul, his sight was restored and he was baptized.

Saul hurriedly packed his bags and escaped, as did Moses, into the desert—not the Sinai, but the sands of Saudi Arabia. There, he spent three years in isolation and anonymity. There, on the backside of the desert, the brash and boastful Saul changed! He had time to meditate on the person of Jesus Christ, to study the Old Testament prophets who had foretold the coming of the Messiah. He had time to relive the brutal way in which the Lord had been dehumanized before and during the Crucifixion. He learned to trust, to obey, and to come to know of the One who was "meek and lowly of heart," not from man, but from the Savior. Saul met love and grace face-to-face in the desert of Arabia and walked out a new man.

Lutheran commentator the late Richard C. H. Linski wrote of Saul's sojourn in Arabia:

Paul's career began, like that of Moses, with flight and with a long period of waiting, waiting, nothing but waiting. This makes the flight from Damascus so significant. It forced Paul into the long wait in which he fully learned he was nothing, that his mightiest asset was utter weakness which enabled God to do everything with him and through him. . . . The tremendous energy of Paul, which at one time made him the worst ravager of the church, which after his conversion sought to make him the mighty disseminator of the gospel, must first of all be humbled in utter weakness and learn the only reliance which was at last learned by Moses: "I will be with thee." (Exod. 3:12; Matt. 28:20.) More may be said; let this suffice.[14]

Immediately upon his return to Damascus Saul began to preach in the synagogues. Soon, danger lurked around every corner, yet the man chosen by God to spread the gospel continued to preach. Early in his ministry, Paul was trapped on the upper floor of a house by a mob of angry men intent on his destruction. The hunter had become the hunted.

When once he marched unhindered through the streets of Damascus, he was now forced to flee. His companions hid Saul in a basket and lowered him to safety through a window.

Saul's next move was to return to Jerusalem, but not to establish the "First Church of the Damascus Road." It would have been the perfect opportunity: Saul had a dramatic testimony of conversion, healing, and deliverance. But no, he simply wished to partner with those who had been in the company of Jesus. Rather than receiving an open-armed reception and a handshake of fellowship, Saul faced fear and rejection. The very men and women who could tell him more of the life of Christ were terrified that there was now a spy in their midst.

Then, from the midst of the fearful believers, one man reached out to Saul:

> But Barnabas took him and brought him to the apostles. And he declared to them how he had seen the Lord on the road, and that He had spoken to him, and how he had preached boldly at Damascus in the name of Jesus. So he was with them at Jerusalem, coming in and going out. And he spoke boldly in the name of the Lord Jesus and disputed against

the Hellenists, but they attempted to kill him.
(Acts 9:27–29 NKJV)

In danger yet again, Saul was urged to escape to Tarsus. Some of his newfound friends helped the apostle find a boat headed in that direction and secured passage for Saul. Perhaps he rejoined his father's tent-making business while he sat on the sidelines in his old hometown. Some Bible scholars opine that Saul spent as many as five years waiting for God to nudge him in a new direction. While he waited, and waited . . . and waited:

> The church had peace throughout Judea, Galilee and Samaria, and grew in strength and numbers. The believers learned how to walk in the fear of the Lord and in the comfort of the Holy Spirit. (Acts 9:31 TLB)

In Tarsus Saul learned dependence, and reappeared with a name change. There is some controversy as to whether God changed Saul's name to Paul or whether the apostle changed his own name, and if so, why. Professor Bill Combs with the Detroit Baptist Theological Seminary wrote:

> In Acts 13:9 . . . Saul sort of officially changed his name at this time. It is suggested

that he decided to give up his Hebrew name Saul in exchange for the name of the illustrious convert of the first missionary journey, Sergius Paulus. But this is clearly not the case.

Paul always had the Latin name *Paullus* (Greek, παυλος) because he was born a Roman citizen (Acts 22:28). Every Roman citizen had three names or *tria nomina*, consisting of a *praenómen* (forename), *nómen* (family name) and *cognómen* (personal name). Most scholars believe that *Paul* is the apostle's *cognomen*. His *praenomen* and *nomen* are unknown. Paul also had another name, a *signum* or *supernomen*—Saul, his Hebrew name. What Luke is telling us is that Paul, "the apostle to the Gentiles" (Rom 11:13), having begun his missionary work to the Gentile world, will now appropriately use his Roman (Gentile) name.[15]

There were scholars in past centuries—and perhaps some even in this present one—who simply could not come to terms with Paul's Damascus Road experience. Oxford scholar Lord George Lyttelton set out to disprove Paul's dramatic conversion. At the end of his studies, Lyttelton determined that Paul's experience was indeed real, that he had really seen the resurrected Lord. In his book *Observations on the Conversion and Apostleship of St. Paul*, Lyttelton shared his conclusions:

- ✧ The conversion and apostleship of St. Paul alone, duly considered, was of itself a demonstration sufficient to prove Christianity to be a divine revelation.

- ✧ [Paul's] zeal was eager and warm, but tempered with prudence, and even with the civilities and decorums of life, as appears by his behavior to Agrippa, Festus and Felix; not the blind, inconsiderate, indecent zeal of an enthusiast.

- ✧ Nothing less than the irresistible evidence of his own senses, clear from all possibility of doubt, could have overcome [Paul's] unbelief.[16]

Many of the men Jesus chose as His inner circle of twelve were simple laborers, and in a sense, that was true of Paul. He was a tentmaker by trade but had been educated under no less than the famed Gamaliel. He spoke Greek, Hebrew, and Aramaic, and his family was steeped in the doctrines and practices of the Pharisees, a trait that made him zealous to protect and defend his religion.

Paul wrote of his background in a letter to the Philippians:

> If someone else thinks they have reasons to put confidence in the flesh, I have more: circumcised on the eighth day, of the people of Israel, of the tribe of Benjamin, a Hebrew of Hebrews; in regard to the law, a Pharisee; as for zeal, persecuting the church; as for righteousness based on the law, faultless. (Philippians 3:4b–6 NIV)

Paul was a Roman citizen and well-acquainted with Greek culture. After his conversion, he would become an equally ardent defender of the faith.

Over the life of his ministry, Paul traveled the Roman world sharing a message of salvation and hope. He preached to Jew and Gentile alike, which alienated many of his listeners, and as a result spent the latter years of his life as a prisoner in Rome. He was ultimately set free by Nero—at least for a time. By the end of his life, Saul of Tarsus, the apostle Paul, had turned what had been considered a small Jewish sect into a force with which to be reckoned. This group of outcasts would ultimately conquer Rome and bring about the conversion of another man, Roman Emperor Constantine. Whether his influence is thought to be good or bad, Constantine made lasting changes that had a great impact on the church, ones that are still felt today.

THE GROWTH OF THE EARLY CHURCH

THE JEWS, under Roman rule, lived very orderly and relatively stable lives. However, those placed in authority over Jerusalem were often greedy and bereft of knowledge of Mosaic law. Because of their lack of understanding, the Romans were prone to confer insult rather than honor. Civil war raged from time to time, launched by Zealots attempting to overthrow Roman rule. The uprisings were often suppressed with massacres that left legions dead.

The last king to rule Judah was Herod Agrippa, the son—or grandson—of Herod. (Herod had been well-known for his incestuous habits, so it is within reason to believe that Agrippa could have been a son.) Although appointed by the Romans to rule the region, Agrippa was identified as a righteous king and frequently received favorable comments. Under his kingship, it appeared that the relationship between the government in Rome and the religionists in Judea had turned a corner and were, at least, harmonious if not overtly friendly.

According to the Jewish Virtual Library:

> The three years of Agrippa's reign were a period of relief and benefit for the Jewish people of Judea. The residents of Jerusalem were exempted from the impost on houses. . . . He omitted the patronymic [surname] "Herod" from coins minted for him and followed a markedly pro-Jewish policy when he was required to arbitrate disputes between Jews and non-Jews . . . Agrippa made frequent changes in the appointment of the high priest. He was highly sympathetic to the Pharisees and was careful to observe Jewish precepts. He married his daughters to Jewish notables, and withdrew his consent to the wedding of one daughter to Antiochus, king of Commagene, when the latter refused to be circumcised.[17]

Sent to Rome as a child, Agrippa became acquainted with a nephew of Augustus Caesar, Gaius Julius Caesar Augustus Germanicus, or, as he was known, Caligula ("little boots," a moniker he despised). The connection between Agrippa and Caligula would later avert a brawl in Judea after the death of Emperor Tiberius. Caligula was known by numerous epithets: mad, insane, unstable, unhinged. He declared himself to be a living god. He had his nephews, who stood between him and the throne of Tiberius, murdered, thereby paving the way to the lofty position of emperor with the blood of his relatives. Caligula was the personification of insanity and his bloody reign one of utter horror. According to author Michael Farquhar, "Caligula had the heads removed from various statues of gods and replaced with his own in some temples."[18]

During his rush to be seen as a living god, Caligula dictated that his statue be placed in the temple in Jerusalem, where the Jews would be required to worship the man. Such a move was guaranteed to spark rebellion in the region: "Accordingly he sent Petronius with an army to Jerusalem to place his statues in the temple, and commanded him that, in case the Jews would not admit of them, he should slay those that opposed it, and carry all the rest into captivity."[19]

Into that quagmire stepped Agrippa. Likely laying his own head on the block, he petitioned Caligula not to move forward with desecrating the Jewish temple. The emperor acquiesced and the order was rescinded, making Jerusalem the only city in the Roman Empire without a statue of Caligula. After approximately four years on the throne in Rome, the emperor's own Praetorian Guard grew tired of his antics and assassinated Caligula.

The Romans were equally brutal toward anyone attempting to foment rebellion in Jewish ranks. Later, after the dispatch of Agrippa, graft and corruption rekindled the fires of Jewish revolt, and finally the Pharisees joined forces with the Zealots. War broke out in the summer of AD 66. Caught off-guard, Roman forces in Judea quickly lost control of the Masada and Antonia fortresses and were slaughtered by the rebels. At Masada rebels discovered a vast quantity of arms and dried food supplies. Herod the Great had stockpiled the materiel more than one hundred years earlier in preparation for a possible war with Cleopatra. The storehouse proved fortuitous, and Jerusalem was soon in Jewish hands.

In Jerusalem the leaders of the rebellion coined money, collected taxes, and organized defenses for the entire country. From Rome, Nero dispatched Roman consul Vespasian with several legions to crush the uprising, the most stubborn and desperate revolt Rome had ever faced. Bloody fighting for the next three years resulted in the isolation of the rebels in Jerusalem and Masada.

Early Christians who had fled Jerusalem were repulsed by the lascivious social mores of the Greeks and Romans and the societies influenced by them. It is probable that the deep divisions between the two entities contributed to the persecution the church faced. The first of the horrific waves of persecution with which early Christians met was said to have been launched by Nero in AD 64. A fire is thought to have started in mid-July and burned for seven devastating days. Three of the fourteen governmental districts in the city were left in ashes while another seven were badly damaged.

Rumors suggesting arson and pointing a finger at Nero as the culprit abounded. That spawned the timeworn saying that "Nero fiddled while Rome burned." One motive that seemed to add gravitas to the accusations that Nero profited from the conflagration was that he seized a vast area of property near the Forum to erect a new palace, the Domus Aurea. Modern historians generally find the accusations to be baseless. Nero had unrestrained power and could do whatever he pleased in the Roman Empire. Why burn what he could take appropriately through what today might be called "eminent domain"? (The power to take private property for public use.)[20]

It was only after the ashes cooled that Nero began to seek a scapegoat to staunch the unfounded rumors. His target of choice: Christians. He issued orders that they be summarily apprehended and slaughtered. Both Peter and Paul were martyred during the reign of Nero. Of their final trial and conviction, little is documented. Author John Pollock wrote of the two disciples:

> Of Paul's final trial, nothing is known beyond a tradition that he was condemned by resolution of the senate on the charge of treason against the divine emperor. How long Simon Peter and Paul were in prison together before being executed the same day, as an early and strong belief asserts, cannot be fixed: possibly as much as nine months. The date honored in the city of their martyrdom is June 29, 67: Peter nailed to a cross as a public spectacle at Nero's Circus on the Vatican, head downward at his own request; and Paul, as a Roman citizen, beheaded in a less public place. [In that instant, Paul's life of hardship,

deprivation, and torture was forgotten as he was welcomed into the arms of his Savior.][21]

Peter and Paul had been caught up in the maelstrom of Nero's conscious decision to heap blame for the great fire that had burned in the city on innocent Christians. Roman historian Cornelius Tacitus wrote of the emperor's ruling:

> Accordingly, an arrest was first made of all who pleaded guilty; then, upon their information, an immense multitude was convicted, not so much of the crime of firing the city, as of hatred against mankind. Mockery of every sort was added to their deaths. Covered with the skins of beasts, they were torn by dogs and perished, or were nailed to crosses, or were doomed to the flames and burnt, to serve as a nightly illumination, when daylight had expired.
>
> Nero offered his gardens for the spectacle, and was exhibiting a show in the circus, while he mingled with the people in the dress of a charioteer or stood aloft on a [cart]. Hence, even for criminals who deserved extreme and exemplary punishment, there arose a feeling

of compassion; for it was not, as it seemed, for the public good, but to glut one man's cruelty, that they were being destroyed.[22]

Rev. Gaylin R. Schmeling, president of Bethany Lutheran Theological Seminary in Minnesota, wrote of those early days of persecution:

> Yet the satanic attack could not crush the church of Christ. The courage of the Christians even in the face of suffering and death for their Savior made a deep impression upon others, and many were converted. Thus the blood of the martyrs became the seed of the church.[23]

Although the early church faced increasing persecution in Rome even after the death of Nero in AD 68, one astonishing prophecy delivered by Jesus in Mark 13:1–4 (NKJV) would soon be fulfilled:

> Then as He went out of the temple, one of His disciples said to Him, "Teacher, see what manner of stones and what buildings are here!" And Jesus answered and said to him, "Do you see these great buildings? Not one stone shall be left upon another, that

shall not be thrown down." Now as He sat
on the Mount of Olives opposite the temple,
Peter, James, John, and Andrew asked Him
privately, "Tell us, when will these things
be? And what will be the sign when all these
things will be fulfilled?"

In AD 70 Vespasian was crowned emperor and returned
to Rome, leaving his son Titus in charge of the Judean campaign. Titus laid siege to Jerusalem with eight thousand
veteran troops. Fewer than a third as many Jews defended
the city. In the face of incredible shortages and starvation,
they clung tenaciously to their city. By late July, Titus had
captured the Antonia Fortress. The defenders who were
hollow-eyed with hunger regrouped. From the roof of the
portico around the edge of the temple platform they hurled
down stones, arrows, and fiery brands against the legion-
naires. The Romans then burned the roofs from under the
Jewish defenders. The attackers gained access to the platform
itself, and the defenders retreated behind the wall of the
temple proper into the Court of the Women and the Court
of Israel. More flaming projectiles set the sanctuary ablaze,
and a bloody slaughter ensued. Biblical scholar Ray Stedman
wrote of that desperate time:

During the long siege a terrible famine raged in the city and the bodies of the inhabitants were literally stacked like cordwood in the streets. Mothers ate their children to preserve their own strength. The toll of Jewish suffering was horrible but they would not surrender the city. Again and again they attempted to trick the Romans through guile and perfidy. When at last the walls were breached Titus tried to preserve the Temple by giving orders to his soldiers not to destroy or burn it. But the anger of the soldiers against the Jews was so intense that, maddened by the resistance they encountered, they disobeyed the order of their general and set fire to the Temple. There were great quantities of gold and silver there which had been placed in the Temple for safekeeping. This melted and ran down between the rocks and into the cracks of the stones. When the soldiers captured the Temple area, in their greed to obtain this gold and silver they took long bars and pried apart the massive stones. Thus, quite literally, [and as had been foretold by Jesus] not one stone was left standing upon another. The Temple itself was totally destroyed, though the wall supporting the area upon which the Temple was built was left partially intact and a portion of it remains to this day, called the Western Wall [or by some, the Wailing Wall].[24]

The Jewish historian Josephus, who had defected to the Romans earlier in the rebellion, was an eyewitness to the event. He claimed that the streams of blood pouring from the corpses of the defenders were more copious than the fire that engulfed everything flammable in the vicinity. Before the Roman legions had finished, the city lay in ruins with the exception of Herod's palace, where the Tenth Legion was stationed as a permanent force of occupation. It would be three more years before the imperial armies recaptured Masada, the last stand of the Jewish revolt. Nearly one thousand men, women, and children had been hiding in this isolated mountaintop fortress. When the Roman soldiers finally scaled the awesome heights and reached the fortress, they were met with an eerie silence. All the Jews at Masada had committed suicide, preferring to die at their own hands than be slaughtered by the armies of Rome.

The destruction of the temple began the second exile. The Diaspora scattered the Jews around the globe for the next eighteen centuries, but there was always a remnant in Jerusalem. Others, although separated from their beloved land, never forgot the Holy City or the destruction of the temple. The cry first went forth, "Next year, Jerusalem."

Judea, prostrate from the war, was slow to recover. Early in the second century, Hadrian, a new emperor, came to the throne. A great administrator, he organized Roman law under a uniform code, sought ways to improve government efficiency, instituted an empire-wide communications system not unlike the Pony Express of the early western United States, and fortified the frontiers. Seeking to unify and strengthen the empire, Hadrian invoked laws to eliminate regional peculiarities. One of these, which prohibited "mutilations," targeted the Jewish practice of circumcision.

During his reign, Hadrian's Wall was built to mark the northern limit of Roman Britain. A substantial portion of the wall still stands. Hadrian also drew up a plan to rebuild Jerusalem as a center of pagan worship and erected temples on Mount Moriah in honor of Jupiter, Juno, and Minerva. Venus's temple was built on Golgotha. The city's name was changed to Aelia Capitolina in honor of the Aelian clan, Hadrian's family. Jews were prohibited from reading the

Torah, partaking of unleavened bread during any of their festivals, and from practicing circumcision. Any infraction was punishable by death.

The new plan saw little progress before it drew a response from Simon Bar-Kokhba, a charismatic Jewish leader. He united the Jews and enticed recruits from throughout the Diaspora, including Samaritans and Gentiles. His troops totaled nearly four hundred thousand when rebellion exploded in AD 132. It took three years and five legions of battle-hardened Roman troops to retake Jerusalem. Bar-Kokhba remained elusive but was eventually captured and executed in AD 136.

After its victory, the Roman army exacted a terrible revenge. Some of the rebel leaders were skinned alive prior to their executions. Massacres during the fighting had been common; now the survivors were either sold into slavery or simply allowed to starve. Burial was not permitted, so heaps of corpses lay decomposing in the streets and fields. The Temple Mount was literally plowed under and an entirely new city was constructed north of the old one. It contained two buildings, together with pagan temples. The temple platform was used as a public square on the south side of the city. It was decked with statues of Hadrian and other Roman notables. An offense punishable by death was established to prevent Jews from entering Jerusalem; neither were they allowed to observe the Sabbath, read or teach the law, circumcise, or otherwise follow God's law.

Hadrian changed the name of Judea to Syria Palaestina and made its capital Caesarea. Jerusalem was no longer the capital city. Syria Palaestina is the origin of the name Palestine and in modern times applies to the area that would eventually become the national homeland of the returning Diaspora Jews. It was said that Hadrian renamed Judea after the ancient enemy of the Jews—the Philistines. Romans in general, and Hadrian in particular, despised Jews.

Of all the nations Romans conquered, the Jewish people were the only group that would never fully submit to the Roman yoke. For that reason, Hadrian was determined to erase the memory of Judea and its people from the pages of history. For the next five hundred years, Jews would only be allowed in the city of Jerusalem on the anniversary of the burning of the temple.

As first the disciples, and then the entire body of believers, began to be persecuted and driven to the uttermost parts of the earth, Christianity was effectively spread outward from Jerusalem. It must have been a bit like the confusion of languages that occurred during the building of what became known as the Tower of Babel. Believers spoke an entirely different language from the rest of the secular world; it was the language of love and loyalty, of prayer and passion, of goodness and grace.

When one views a map of the early apostolic journeys, it is easily discernable that the geographic focus was on Asia Minor, or modern-day Turkey. Cities named in the Pauline Epistles were Ephesus, Colossae, and Galatia. In his first letter, Peter wrote of journeys to Cappadocia, Bithynia, Asia, Pontus, and Galatia. John the Revelator included the seven churches located in Ephesus, Smyrna, Pergamum, Thyatira, Sardis, Philadelphia, and Laodicea. Sadly, this region fell to the Turks (Muslims) about AD 1,000. It has not been predominately Christian since that time.

Persecution in the early church could, perhaps, be attributed to the chasm between its principles and the profligacy of pagan society. Christian apologist and early church father, Tertullian, questioned the rush to judgment of Christians:

> We have nothing to do with the madness of the Cirque [circus], with the obsceneness of the stage, and the cruelty of the amphitheatre, and the vanity of the Xystus [a large gallery or portico planted about with trees,

where the athletes performed in the winter time]. The Epicurean sect is tolerated in the exercise of their pleasures, and why are we such intolerable offenders for non-conforming with you in point of pleasure?[25]

Perhaps one of the best-known martyrs of the second century was Polycarp, the bishop of Smyrna, who died in AD 155. He had been a student under the teachings of John the apostle. Some Bible scholars believe it was Polycarp to whom the letter to the church in Smyrna was addressed. In it, John issued a warning:

Do not fear any of those things which you are about to suffer. Indeed, the devil is about to throw some of you into prison, that you may be tested, and you will have tribulation ten days. Be faithful until death, and I will give you the crown of life. (Revelation 2:10 NKJV)

Polycarp's martyrdom brought perhaps his greatest impact on the early church. He lived between AD 70 and 155, a time of great persecution and vicious assaults against Christians. The elder Polycarp was detained simply for being a member of the doctrinally dangerous cult of Christianity.

Fearing its rapid growth, officials in Rome were determined to stamp it out. Having pity on the old man standing before him in chains, the Roman proconsul offered Polycarp a way of escape: simply avow, "Caesar is Lord." His response instead was said to be:

> Eighty-six years I have served Christ, and He never did me any wrong. How can I blaspheme my King who saved me?[26]

Tradition has it that once inside the arena, Polycarp was given a second opportunity to swear an oath of loyalty to Caesar; again he declined. The Christian statesman was spared death by ravenous beasts due to a brief moratorium of that event; Polycarp was instead burned alive at the stake.

What prompted such oppression and harassment? As with their Jewish counterparts, Christians were frequently charged with cannibalism based on the celebration of the Last Supper where Jesus broke the bread and then instructed His followers to "Take, eat; this is my body." Followers of Christ also refused to participate in ritual sacrifices to Roman deities. This was a direct frontal assault against the gods thought to protect the Roman Empire, thus placing it in grave danger. Repudiating the practice of bowing down to

Roman emperors who were proclaimed gods was seen as both blasphemy and sedition. What better way to determine if a person was truly a follower of Christ than to compel him/her to swear allegiance by offering a sacrifice to the emperor?

CRUEL & COLD-BLOODED CUSTODIANS OF ROME

IN THE PANTHEON of Roman emperors, Nero was succeeded by Galba in AD 68. He relinquished the throne to Otho, and then Vitellius in a matter of only a few months. These three short-lived rulers were followed by Vespasian and then his son, Titus, who ruled from AD 69–81, under whom the Christian population had a respite. Author John Carlin wrote of the two leaders:

> There are no indications that Christians were attacked or persecuted in any way by these two emperors. During their reigns (12 years) the Church of Rome flourished and experienced a period of peace and tranquility.

In fact, many converts in Rome came from the highest circles of the imperial society. Flavius Sabinus, elder brother of Vespasian, became a Christian as did his son Flavius Clemens. Clemens' wife and two sons also converted and his wife donated land for a Christian cemetery in Rome that exists to this day.[27]

In AD 81 Domitian, Vespasian's son, burst on the scene following the death of his brother Titus. Some historians conjecture that Domitian may have helped his brother to his death. Alas, the breather that had been afforded Christians ended; persecution would return in full measure under the rule of that brutal and sadistic killer. Journalist Mark Galli wrote of what one early church chronicler thought of Domitian:

> The historian Pliny called Domitian the beast from hell who sat in its den, licking blood. In the Book of Revelation, John of the Apocalypse may have referred to Domitian when he described a beast from the abyss who blasphemes heaven and drinks the blood of the saints.[28]

In his work *Panegyricus*, Pliny the Younger, an attorney and author, also had the following to say about the emperor:

> He [Domitian] was a madman, blind to the true meaning of his position, who used the arena for collecting charges of high treason, who felt himself slighted and scorned if we failed to pay homage to his gladiators, taking any criticism of them to himself and seeing insults to his own godhead and divinity; who deemed himself the equal of the gods yet raised his gladiators to his equal.[29]

Domitian was said to have been a master architect and skillful bureaucrat who adroitly oversaw local administrators and regional authorities. Underlying that managerial proficiency was a cruel and merciless individual. It has been said of him that he enjoyed inflicting pain on the lowliest creatures, but was equally thrilled to watch women and dwarves fight to the death in the gladiatorial arena. Domitian's court was rife with spies because of his unhealthy fear of subversive schemes against him.

Most Roman emperors had to wait until after death to be deified; Domitian was unwilling to prolong his elevation to godlike status. He egotistically had himself declared "God the Lord" and insisted that those he encountered proclaim his greatness. Epithets such as "holy" and "invincible" greeted him in the streets and marketplace. Both Christians and Jews in the realm balked at the use of those words in conjunction with Domitian. As a result, persecution proliferated once again. He had Christians exiled and/or executed. What Domitian had discounted was that someone would have the temerity to beat him at his own monstrous game. Stephanus, the ex-slave of a Christian who had been ordered executed, marshaled a group of Domitian's adversaries who unceremoniously assassinated the emperor.

The succession of emperors following Domitian, among them Trajan and Marcus Aurelius, did little to stem the tide of persecution heaped upon Jew and Christian alike. Trajan's rule was focused on conquest. His desire was to surpass the successes of his idol, Julius Caesar, an aspiration that failed dismally. Trajan's only notable invasion was that of Dacia, a region in central Europe bounded by the Carpathian Mountains. It was the last territorial subjugation of the Roman Empire. Trajan was a prolific advocate for public works—aqueducts, baths, and finally, the splendid Forum of Trajan financed by the spoils gathered from the defeat of Dacia.

Yet this leader who did so much good for Rome was

among those emperors that persecuted Christians. He is said to have written to Governor Pliny of Bithynia:

> They [Christians] are not to be hunted out. [Although] any who are accused and convicted should be punished, with the proviso that if a man says he is not a Christian and makes it obvious by his actual conduct—namely, by worshiping our gods—then, however suspect he may have been with regard to the past, he should gain pardon from his repentance.[30]

The emperor Trajan was thought to have been the first Roman ruler to persecute Christians as a separate sect from the Jews. Ignatius, bishop of Antioch and a student of the apostle John, was perhaps the best known to have suffered martyrdom during the reign of Trajan. (It was in Antioch that Christ's followers were first called "Christians" Acts 11:26.)

Another emperor that fueled anti-Christian resentment was Marcus Aurelius. As a leader, he practiced humanity toward the weak and helpless—unless, of course, they were Christians. He believed them to be a subversive group, a treacherous and radical faction that was both vulgar and depraved. Marcus Aurelius encouraged the distribution of anti-Christian writings. Such missives fostered persecution within the confines of the Roman Empire and led to the execution of the Bishop of Lyons and of Justin, a Christian philosopher. An account of Justin's trial was preserved:

> The Prefect Rusticus says: Approach and sacrifice, all of you, to the gods. Justin says: No one in his right mind gives up piety for impiety. The Prefect Rusticus says: If you do not obey, you will be tortured without mercy. Justin replies: That is our desire, to be tortured for Our Lord, Jesus Christ, and so to be saved, for that will give us salvation and firm confidence at the more terrible universal tribunal of Our Lord and Saviour. And all the martyrs said: Do as you wish; for we are Christians, and we do not sacrifice to idols. The Prefect Rusticus read the sentence: Those who do not wish to sacrifice to the gods and to obey the emperor will be scourged and beheaded according to the laws. The holy martyrs glorifying God betook themselves to the customary place, where they were

beheaded and consummated their martyrdom confessing their Saviour.[31]

Sporadic persecution of Christians in Rome continued for the next century, but it was in the third century that even more intense torture and suffering ensued—though not empire-wide. Bridging the century from the second to the third was Septimus Severus, who was first, last, and always the model soldier. He began his ascent to the throne in AD 193 and, while consolidating his rule in Rome, raised the pay of soldiers 67 percent. He also elevated their functions in the empire so that a career in the military became a positive track for engaging in various professions.

Initially, Emperor Severus was sympathetic toward the Christian population. It is said that his son, Caracalla, was raised by a Christian nurse. By 202, however, an event or perhaps some person changed his regard for Judaism and Christianity. He, then, directed that conversions to either religion be halted, and instigated persecutions, especially in Northern Africa. Under Severus's direction and with his blessing, faithful followers such as Leonides, father of Origen, biblical scholar and philosopher, was beheaded for his faith. So determined was Origen to follow in his father's footsteps that Eusebius records:

Almighty God used his mother to defeat his
ambition. She first appealed to him in words,
begging him to spare his mother's feelings for
him; then, when the news that his father had
been arrested and imprisoned filled his whole
being with a craving for martyrdom, and she
saw that he was more determined than ever,
she hid all his clothing and compelled him
to stay home. . . . This may serve as the first
evidence of Origen's boyish sagacity and the
perfect sincerity of his devotion to God.[32]

The persecution abated upon the death of Severus in
AD 211. For over three decades, the Christian population
enjoyed a respite, but in AD 249, Decius rose to the rank
of emperor. Fearing the weakening of traditional thinking,
Decius recognized the military dimensions of the problem
but perceived some spiritual ones as well.

Concerned that traditional worship of multiple deities
would be overrun by Christian theology, Decius instigated a
resurrection of religious zeal for deified Roman rulers, which
he thought would aid in the restoration of Rome's past glory.
Only one group stood in his way: Christians who believed in
the worship of the one true God. As a result Decius reinstated

the practice of persecuting believers throughout the Roman Empire. Historically, the first martyr to die following the edict by Decius was Fabian, Bishop of Rome.

According to Dan Graves, author and researcher:

> In Rome, there is an old slab of stone that is special. On it, worn Greek letters are still visible. Translated, they read, "Fabian, bishop, martyr." Fabian had been the Bishop of Rome (Pope) for fourteen years when the Roman Emperor Decius made up his mind to smash the unpopular Christian church. On . . . January 20, 250, the prominent and holy Fabian died for his faith.[33]

Decius introduced a measure whereby Christians were required to engage in a single pagan ritual. Compliance would afford them a "Certificate of Sacrifice" that cleared them of religious treason. Its purpose: to ensure religious harmony in the Roman Empire. Of course, there were some Christians who bowed to the demand of Decius; others bribed officials to fraudulently acquire a certificate. But there were those devout believers who refused to concede and chose instead to face a martyr's death.

During that period, Origen was detained by the Roman

Guard and savagely tortured. He was eventually released but died not many years thereafter, not a martyr, but a confessor of the faith.

Decius died in AD 251 but not before presenting his successors with a blueprint for persecution that would be fully invoked under Emperor Diocletian in the early fourth century. Before Diocletian sat on the throne, there was Valerian, who ruled from AD 253 to 260.

The new emperor had fallen heir to an empire rampant with strife and disease. Germanic tribes from the east had successfully and efficiently raided that region with confidence that the Romans were spread too thin to properly repel the invaders. Northern tribes were also making inroads into the crumbling Roman Empire. Valerian quickly realized that something must be done to defend his kingdom. First, he appointed his son, Licinius Egnatius Gallienus, as co-ruler. Second, he adopted the strategy of diversion used by other emperors before him: He blamed the Christians for the chaos in the realm.

Expanding the policies of Decius, Valerian ordered clerics to make sacrificial offerings to the gods of Rome. Soon thereafter, Valerian declared that the clergy were subject to the death penalty. Pope Stephen I, Pope Sixtus II, and Lawrence of Rome, one of seven deacons who served under the pope, were summarily executed. Outside Rome Cyprian, the Bishop of Carthage, was banished from his post, but that was not to be the least of his persecution:

> When a year had passed he [Cyprian] was recalled and kept practically a prisoner in his own villa, in expectation of severe measures after a new and more stringent imperial edict arrived, demanding the execution of all Christian clerics, according to reports of it by Christian writers.
>
> On September 13, 258, he was imprisoned at the behest of the new proconsul, Galerius Maximus. The day following he was examined for the last time and sentenced to die by the sword. His only answer was "Thanks be to God!" The execution was carried out at once in an open place near the city. A vast multitude followed Cyprian on his last journey. He removed his garments without assistance, knelt down, and prayed. After he blindfolded himself, he was beheaded by the sword.[34]

The lands, houses, and personal property of Christian

congregations were confiscated and the individuals sentenced to hard labor in the mines.

In AD 259 while repelling a Persian attack in Mesopotamia, Valerian was captured. Author Michael Grant in his book *The Roman Emperors: A Biographical Guide to the Rulers of Imperial Rome, 31 B.C. – A.D. 476* wrote of the emperor's capture. He said of Valerian's ignominious end, "For the capture of an emperor by a foreign foe was an unparalleled catastrophe, the nadir of Roman disgrace."[35] Valerian's arrest and subsequent execution led ultimately to the lifting of all edicts issued against Christians.

But again, the short respite for believers in the empire was ended by Diocletian, who ruled the Roman Empire from 284 to 305. He was said to have been a gifted organizer whose administrative abilities led, once again, directly to the Christian population. Persecution was the order of the day, and despite the fact that Diocletian's wife, Prisca, was a believer, the emperor seemed determined to destroy all the Christians in the empire. (Tolerant coexistence is a decidedly new theory, and certainly not one that was rampant in Rome in the third and fourth centuries—and especially as it might relate to Christians.)

Diocletian's first directive was to obliterate theological libraries and halt worship by believers. Once again, the clergy was threatened with arrest unless they were willing to make a sacrifice to the heathen gods of Rome. Those laws were particularly cruel and brutal on the African continent. In AD 304, the emperor was stricken with an acute, unnamed malady and abdicated. He retired to his farm in Dalmatia (now Yugoslavia). By 311, persecution of Christians was once more halted, and the following year, Constantine emerged as leader. His rule would change Christianity forever.

The apostle Paul warned the early church the consequences of taking their focus off Christ and allowing secularism to seep in:

> I know that after I leave, savage wolves will come in among you and will not spare the flock. Even from your own number men will arise and distort the truth in order to draw away disciples after them. (Acts 20:29–30 NIV)

Peter was also swift to warn the church of coming danger:

> But there were also false prophets among the people, even as there will be false teachers among you, who will secretly bring in destructive heresies, even denying the Lord who bought them, and bring on themselves

swift destruction. And many will follow their destructive ways, because of whom the way of truth will be blasphemed. By covetousness they will exploit you with deceptive words; for a long time their judgment has not been idle, and their destruction does not slumber. (2 Peter 2:1–3 NKJV)

FLAVIUS VALERIUS CONSTANTINUS, EMPEROR

THE MAN WHO would become known as Roman emperor Constantine I was born between AD 272 and 284 (reported birth dates vary) in what is now Niš, Serbia. His father, at the time, served in the army of Rome. It is unknown if his mother, Helena, was a wife or mistress of his father, Constantius. Her standing was of little importance, as Helena was abandoned in favor of the stepdaughter of Maximian, the man who ruled over the Western Roman Empire. It was a fortuitous move on the part of Constantius. In AD 293, he was elevated to the role of Deputy Emperor. It was a position that made it possible to send his son, Constantine, to the Eastern Roman Empire to study Latin and Greek in the court of Diocletian. It is highly likely that during his studies, Constantine witnessed the heinous persecution of Christians in the empire.

In 305, Diocletian decreed that both he and Maximian would retire—much to the latter's chagrin. Author James Carroll wrote:

> Diocletian, sixty years old, abdicated the imperial throne—probably a signal of his serious purpose as a reforming ruler. He imposed the same decision on Maximian, his counterpart in the West. Constantius and Galerius became Augusti [official title of a Roman emperor]. . . . Constantius was still more the rough soldier than the courtly emperor; soon after his ascension to the rank of Augustus, he led his legions into Britain to maintain control over the island's perennially unruly natives. While there, in 305, Constantius was taken ill. He died at York. At his side was his son Constantine.[36]

Having impressed the troops that served under his father, the eighteen-year-old Constantine was spontaneously declared successor. Maximian, who had taken up residence in Rome, rose up in opposition to again declare his leadership role as emperor over the Western region of the empire.

The young Constantine refused to kowtow to the former emperor and began to execute his plan to consolidate leadership in the empire. Civil war soon followed. Constantine took control in the northern reaches of the empire and as his first order of business had the imposing palace—Konstantin Basilika—erected in Trier. He also began to formulate a battle strategy to remove Maximian, his father-in-law, from the throne. In a bold move to assure his continued reign, the threatened leader traveled to Trier to meet with Constantine. The wily young leader quickly recognized Maximian as the senior Augustus and confirmed the agreement by marrying Fausta, his daughter.

A year later, Maxentius, only son of the senior Augustus, belatedly realized that he was being forced aside, and established a claim to the title of Emperor of the Western Roman Empire. The father, of course, sided with the son, and amassed his troops for a battle with Constantine at Marseilles in AD 310. The outcome was favorable to Constantine's army, which slew Maximian. Two years later, Constantine marched through Italy to face the army of Maximius, who was ensconced in Rome. Thus is born the following story of Constantine's conversion to Christianity.

Surrounded by an army disheartened and homesick, the decided underdogs in the upcoming fray, Constantine faced a long night of self-examination. As he camped with his troops along the Tiber near the Milvian Bridge, it is said that the embattled emperor had a vision. In the sky, a cross appeared above the Latin inscription *In Hoc Signo Vinces* or "In this sign, conquer." Constantine was directed in his vision "to mark the heavenly sign of God on the shields of his soldiers. . .by means of a slanted letter X with the top of its head bent round, he marked Christ on their shields."[37] (This is also recognized as the first two letters of the Greek alphabet, *Chi*, an X and *Rho the letter* P.) News of the vision roused his troops, lifting them from their lethargy and sending them courageously into battle the following morning. Constantine positioned his smaller army the length of his foe's hordes, deployed his cavalry against that of Maxentius, and ordered his infantry to march forward. When the two forces clashed, the army of Maxentius was summarily pushed into the Tiber, where the men either died by the sword or drowned in the river. As he attempted to cross the bridge his men had built from boats, Maxentius was ignominiously forced into the river where he, too, drowned.

Historians conjecture that the course of Constantine's

conversion posed difficulties. He quickly proclaimed that both Christians and pagans would be permitted to worship unhindered and almost as hastily returned property appropriated by his predecessors. He moved to restore other privileges that had been forbidden, but those measures did nothing to assure a Christian approach to government. Paganism was still the order of the day as Constantine directed that a new city be built in his honor: Constantinople. The politically correct narrative for that ploy was to construct a capital befitting the monarch's conversion, which only left the wordsmiths of that day with the problem of explaining why this newly erected Christian city was filled with pagan temples and sculptures.

In an attempt to be more understanding of the situation, could it be that perhaps Constantine had not yet been taught the Way? Likely he did not comprehend that the followers of Jesus Christ were monotheistic and not polytheistic. The adherents of Christianity were expected to devote themselves totally and exclusively to the tenets of the gospel. To give him credit, he turned not to the gods of Rome or Greece, but to the Great I Am.

In AD 313, the Edict of Milan was signed by the two Augusti who had met on the occasion of the wedding of Constantine's sister. The document proclaimed:

When I, Constantine Augustus, as well as
I Licinius Augustus d fortunately met near
Mediolanurn (Milan), and were considering
everything that pertained to the public wel-
fare and security, we thought, among other
things which we saw would be for the good
of many, those regulations pertaining to the
reverence of the Divinity ought certainly
to be made first, so that we might grant to
the Christians and others full authority to
observe that religion which each preferred;
whence any Divinity whatsoever in the seat
of the heavens may be propitious and kindly
disposed to us and all who are placed under
our rule[.] And thus by this wholesome coun-
sel and most upright provision we thought
to arrange that no one whatsoever should
be denied the opportunity to give his heart
to the observance of the Christian religion,
of that religion which he should think best
for himself, so that the Supreme Deity, to
whose worship we freely yield our hearts
may show in all things His usual favor and
benevolence.[38]

In AD 320 Licinius, son of Valerian, had second thoughts about his support for the Edict of Milan and began to harass Christians in the regions under his control. His decrees became less favorable as Christians were ousted from their jobs, property was again confiscated, and his rule became definitely more anti-Christian. Licinius determined that the Christian element in the empire was more devoted to Constantine because of his conversion.

His paranoia finally led Licinius to engage Goth mercenaries, paid warriors with no loyalty to a king or cause; they fought only for personal enrichment. Finally in 324, Constantine led his armies into Thrace, the only region over which Licinius exerted leadership. The troops faced each other in Adrianople, and although Constantine's army was outnumbered by that of their opponent, they were battle-hardened and more zealous for their cause. Although Licinius was spared, in September of that same year, he and the commander of his bodyguard surrendered. The Roman Empire was once again united under the rule of one man—Constantine. Licinius was forced to live as a private citizen in Thessalonica. In 325 he and his son were hanged for treason.

In the early years of the fourth century, Arius, a priest in Alexandria, Egypt, began to teach that Christ, the Son of God, was not divine but simply a created being like all other men. Bishop Alexander opposed that doctrine, and the ensuing debate loomed over the church and threatened the future of the Roman Empire.

With the empire consolidated under his rule, Constantine summoned heads of the church to a meeting at Nicaea (now Isnik in Turkey). Constantine's summons read:

> That there is nothing more honorable in my sight than the fear of God, is, I believe, manifest to every man. . . . Wherefore I signify to you, my beloved brethren, that all of you promptly assemble at the said city, that is at Nicaea. Let everyone of you therefore, regarding that which is best, as I said before, be diligent, without delay in anything, speedily to come, that he may be in his own person present as a spectator of those things which will be done by the same.
>
> God keep you my beloved brethren.[39]

James, the brother of Jesus, the overseer of Jerusalem, had established an organization of elders in the church. Those elders were in charge of bishops. It was that hierarchal structure in which Constantine saw a parallel to the Roman

Empire. It was to those leaders that he issued an invitation to Nicaea. The bishops in attendance had been called from the far reaches of the empire and included men from the Eastern Orthodox Church and the Coptic Orthodox Church of Alexandria. Author Simon Sebag Montifiore said of the significance of the meeting:

> It was at Nicaea . . . that Macarius, the Bishop of Aelia Capitolina (once called Jerusalem), brought the fate of his small and neglected town to Constantine's attention. Constantine knew Aelia . . . Now keen to celebrate his success at Nicaea and project the sacred glory of his empire, he decided to restore the city and create what Eusebius (Bishop of Caesarea and the emperor's biographer) called 'The New Jerusalem built over against the one so famous of old'. Constantine commissioned a church that befitted Jerusalem as the cradle of the Good News.[40]

It was during this meeting that the bishops agreed—mostly—on a prescribed statement of beliefs, and specifically on how Jesus Christ is God.

In an attempt to disavow the heresy introduced by Arius,

the word *homoousios,* translated "of the same essence," was included in the sacrament of baptism. It was thought the inclusion of that particular word would affirm unequivocally that Christ was a member of the Godhead, and as such was divine.

Attendance figures at Nicaea vary from 300 to 318 with an untold number of acolytes and assistants accompanying the various leaders. The Council approved the measure unanimously, with only three dissenting bishops: Arius, Theonas, and Secundus. In accordance with Constantine's edict, the three men were exiled to Illyria and excommunicated. All works attributed to Arius were ordered seized and burned and those in possession of the banned writings were to be slain.

The Nicaean Creed was revised in 381. Some Christian churches even today continue to utter the Nicene Creed, not as an oath of loyalty to Constantine, but as a religious exercise. The Creed, as adopted in 325, declared:

> We believe in one God, the Father, the Almighty, maker of heaven and earth, of all that is, seen and unseen.
>
> We believe in one Lord, Jesus Christ, the only Son of God, eternally begotten of the

Father, God from God, Light from Light, true God from true God, begotten, not made, of one Being with the Father. Through him all things were made. For us and for our salvation he came down from heaven: by the power of the Holy Spirit he became incarnate from the Virgin Mary, and was made man. For our sake he was crucified under Pontius Pilate; he suffered death and was buried. On the third day he rose again in accordance with the Scriptures; he ascended into heaven and is seated at the right hand of the Father. He will come again in glory to judge the living and the dead, and his kingdom will have no end.

We believe in the Holy Spirit, the Lord, the giver of life, who proceeds from the Father. With the Father and the Son he is worshiped and glorified. He has spoken through the Prophets. We believe in one holy catholic and apostolic Church. We acknowledge one baptism for the forgiveness of sins. We look for the resurrection of the dead, and the life of the world to come. Amen.[41]

Constantine's vision of the cross, which would ultimately become a symbol of veneration rather than one of cruel brutality, and the implementation of the Nicene Creed unified the church. Eusebius bestowed even more gravitas on Constantine with his belief that "the (Christian) Emperor is God's representative on earth, and as the Word of God expressed God's will in the creation of the world, so the Emperor expresses the will of God in the government of the civilized world (the oikoumene), and fulfills this role by his imitation of the Word."[42]

It was Constantine's discourse at Nicaea that launched his mother, Helena, on a pilgrimage in 326 in search of the actual cross of Christ in Jerusalem. Pastor Carolyn Dipboye of Grace Covenant Church, Oakridge, Tennessee, wrote of the change in how we view the cross:

> I recall the horror that greeted Larry's [her husband, Pastor Larry Dipboye] suggestion some years ago that the beauty we associate with the cross would have been foreign to early Christians who knew the cross for what it was—an instrument of torture and shame. The *ichthys,* the sacred fish whose letters formed the acrostic of "Jesus Christ, Son of

God, Savior," is prominent in early Christian symbolism and art, as are palm branches, the dove, the peacock and the Chi Rho (the first two letters of the Greek word for Christ), but not the cross [James Carroll, *Constantine's Sword*, 174–175]. Larry went on to suggest that we might understand the repulsion early Christians felt to the cross if we imagined the state's primary instrument of torture and death of our day, the electric chair, crafted in gold and bejeweled as a piece of jewelry to hang around our necks. A near riot ensued.[43]

The early church did not use the symbol of the cross, because the cross was thought to be a despicable representation. A form of execution that originated with the Persians and was later adopted by the Romans, crucifixion was designed to humiliate a person and bring a slow, excruciating death. The cross also served as a warning to anyone who saw it that they had better not mess with Rome. The sight of a man surrounded by Roman guards and carrying a cross through the streets meant that he was about to die a slow and painful death.

Greg Laurie, author and pastor, wrote:

Today the cross has lost its meaning. For many, it is little more than a fashion accessory. Like the woman in the jewelry store who asked to see the crosses "without this little man on them," many people today are looking for a cross without Jesus, one that requires nothing from them. But if we are to be followers of Jesus, then we must take up the cross.[44]

The woman most responsible for changing the way people saw the cross was Helena, mother of Constantine. She disappeared from public view after having been divorced by Constantius. When her son became emperor, Helena reappeared and was given the title Flavia Julia, Helena Augusta. She was reverently designated *nobilissima femina*, or "most noble lady." That label, along with *divi Constanti castissimae coniugi*, or "most chaste wife of the late emperor Constantius" was thought to have been bestowed upon her to dismiss gossip that she was but a concubine of the Emperor Constantius.[45] Constantine presented his mother with the *Sessorium*, a royal dwelling located outside the walls of Rome. Helena then did what many new homeowners do: She set about redecorating and updating the royal residence.

Eusebius wrote that Helena was converted to Christianity by her son. Did her conversion come before or after she supposedly implicated her daughter-in-law in the death of Crispus, Constantine's firstborn son? Crispus, the son of a concubine, was highly favored for his military exploits. He had battled alongside his father during several campaigns. But, alas, poor Crispus! As one writer opined, he was to die an ignominious death:

> Although many rumours exist, the exact reason remains unknown. All that is certain is that Constantine executed Crispus in 326, at the tender age of twenty-one. Fausta may have played a large part in this incident by poisoning Constantine's mind against Crispus.
>
> Sometime after the execution, Constantine realized his mistake. It was likely that his mother Helena, rather than the wife of Crispus, persuaded him of his son's innocence. But it was too late for regrets. Constantine could only erect a golden statue in memory of his dead son. His conscience probably found some solace knowing that God forgave him and still loved him. But his son Crispus

would never return to life again because of his mistake.

As the closest person to Constantine, Fausta probably knew her husband very well. She would have known his doubts and insecurities. Therefore she could easily manipulate him into believing that Crispus harboured ill-intent against him. Her motives were simple. As long as Crispus lived, he would always pose a threat to her sons.

Exactly what Fausta said is unknown, although there are many theories. One tale suggests she loved Crispus but he showed no interest. Due to the humiliation, she told Constantine that Crispus attempted to rape her. Another tale alleges that she accused Crispus of forcing a girl to be his concubine. She knew full well that Constantine abhorred such inappropriate sexual relations. However Fausta convinced Constantine, the fact remains she managed to get Crispus killed.[46]

Fausta's machinations would not go far to secure the empire for her offspring. It is said that after the demise of Crispus, Helena persuaded Constantine that Fausta was responsible for the death of his son. Overcome with contrition, Constantine placed the blame for his blood-thirsty frenzy on his wife and had her executed. Accounts of her demise vary by historian; one says she was boiled alive, another that she was suffocated, and yet another that she died by her own hand by order of the emperor. What can be said with accuracy is that however she perished, it was at the command of her husband, the emperor.

Soon after the burial of her grandson and daughter-in-law, Helena, the septuagenarian, set off on a journey to the Holy Land. She approached each hallowed site along the way very publicly in order to reinforce the occupation of the area and its oversight by her son, Constantine. Her pilgrimage was very much a royal tour with all its pomp and trappings. During visits to various holy sites, she offered praise to God for Emperor Constantine's conversion. Her route would take Helena through Syria and into Jerusalem where she planned to visit the various churches erected by order of her son.

As she traveled the dusty roads of the Middle East, she provided assistance to those less fortunate. She was described by Eusebius as follows:

MIKE EVANS

Especially abundant were the gifts she bestowed on the naked and unprotected poor. To some she gave money, to others an ample supply of clothing; she liberated some from imprisonment, or from the bitter servitude of the mines; others she delivered from unjust oppression, and others again, she restored from exile. While, however, her character derived luster from such deeds. . .she was far from neglecting personal piety toward God. She might be seen continually frequenting His Church, while at the same time she adorned the houses of prayer with splendid offerings, not overlooking the churches of the smallest cities. In short, this admirable woman was to be seen, in simple and modest attire, mingling with the crowd of worshipers, and testifying her devotion to God by a uniform course of pious conduct (*The Life of Constantine*, XLIV, XLV).[47]

Upon reaching Antioch, Helena discovered that her welcome was less than stellar because of a disagreement with the bishop, Eustathius. Some historians believe it was a theological issue; that he lamented the lowly birth of the mother of Constantine. Discrimination was indeed alive and well in fourth century Rome.

As the "most pious augusta," Helena's virtue and faithfulness in church attendance, and the endowments to various places of worship were to be revered, certainly not questioned. She visited her son's various church-building sites that could be found in Mamre, the place where God visited Abraham (Genesis 18:1); in Bethlehem, the birthplace of Jesus; and on the Mount of Olives. The cathedrals were later dedicated by Constantine in honor of his then-deceased mother.

Although Jews had been forbidden to enter Jerusalem, Gentile Christians were welcomed. Consequently, members of the church who had all but disappeared from the city after AD 70 began to reappear there. Sometime in the second century, the first church building was erected on Mount Zion. Under Constantine, Jerusalem suddenly began to regain prestige. He sent funds to the Holy City to be used to excavate and preserve Christian relics and sites. In addition, Helena also saw to the demolition of the temple of Aphrodite. It was on the site of that pagan temple that, as tradition holds, Jesus had been buried after the crucifixion; thus the origin of the Church of the Holy Sepulchre built in AD 335.

The culmination of Helena's life was the legend that she had discovered the "True Cross" on which Jesus had died. A. R. Birley wrote of the relic:

> The increased reverence for the Cross as a symbol of Christian belief during the Constantinian period naturally played a role here. But neither the author of the Pilgrimage from Bordeaux of A.D. 333, nor Eusebius, who died in A.D. 339, refers to relics of the Cross. The former mentions only the rock of Golgotha, the Holy Sepulchre, and the new basilica of Constantine. All the same, a few years later the bishop of Jerusalem, Cyril, refers several times in his *Cathechetical Lectures* (A.D. 350) to pieces of wood from the cross being already scattered around the Mediterranean lands. Certainly, as early as A.D. 359 a church in Mauretania had a collection of relics which included a fragment of the cross. Further, Cyril, in his letter to Constantius II, explicitly dates the discovery of the cross to the reign of Constantine, when, through the favour of God, 'the holy places which had been hidden were revealed'.[48]

Historians believe that Helena died not long after she returned from her sojourn to the Holy Land at the approximate age of eighty. She was laid to rest in a mausoleum on the *Via Labicana* outside Rome. In the eleventh century, Helena's sarcophagus, originally carved for her son Constantine, was removed from the mausoleum and now rests in the museums of the Vatican. As unlikely as it is that Helena discovered the cross of Christ, it was on that premise that the Eastern Orthodox and Roman Catholic churches conferred sainthood upon her.

APOSTASY ARISES

THE FOURTH-CENTURY adoption of the Nicene Creed set a course for change in the church that still resonates in the twenty-first century. Following his conversion, Constantine embraced Christianity as the approved religion in the Roman Empire. His personal life seemed little changed by his decision, as the life of the emperor continued to be overshadowed by scandal and carnage. At the same time, the prelates in Rome gained power both in the political and secular realms.

Even though he had pledged his allegiance to the Christian church, Constantine continued to dabble in sun worship and other pagan practices. The marriage of biblical faith with that of paganism was accomplished so furtively, few took note when the day of rest and worship had been changed from Saturday, as followed by the Jews. Constantine had issued a decree on March 7, 321, ordering the Romans to observe Sunday as the day of rest:

> On the venerable Day of the Sun let the magistrates and people residing in cities rest, and let all workshops be closed. In the country, however, persons engaged in agriculture may freely and lawfully continue their pursuits; because it often happens that another day is not so suitable for grain-sowing or vine-planting; lest by neglecting the proper moment for such operations the bounty of heaven should be lost.[49]

As would often become the case with new converts to the Church of Rome, pagan practices would be so smoothly incorporated into its rituals they would soon become indistinguishable to believers. James Carroll, author of *Constantine's Sword*, wrote:

> The potent movement toward monotheism among pagans is reflected in the fact that *Summus Deus* was by then a commanded Roman form of address to the deity. As seen in

Constantine's originating piety, that supreme deity would have been associated with the sun, and pagans would have recognized, with reason, their own solar cult in such Christian practices as orienting churches to the east, worshiping on "sun day," and celebrating the birth of the deity at the winter solstice.

That Christian piety commonly included pagan practice and superstition would have been part of the broad appeal of the Gospel among the least educated. Constantine's famously converted army, for example, was made up of unlettered peasants and barbarians. . . . the cross of Christ as the standard to march behind would have evoked the ancestral totem of the sacred tree far more powerfully than it would have Saint Paul's token of deliverance. Such an association may have figured in Constantine's instinctive grasp of the cross as a sign to rally to, since his army of barbarians, which grew with every conquest, as the first population he had to unify. Beginning with that army, a pragmatic tolerance, up to a point, would have been Constantine's modus operandi.[50]

Rather than object to the emperor's move, the Roman Church accepted it and began to solidify its own position by announcing that Peter, not Christ, was head of the church. It was a move not totally supported by Paul's letter to the Ephesians, which stated unequivocally: ". . . let us grow in every way into Him who is the head—Christ" (Ephesians 4:15 HCSB).

Would Peter have ever viewed himself as the titular head of the church? No one disciple held that role in the years after Christ's ascension. Ephesians 2:19–20 (NKJV) clearly reveals just who is the authority in the church:

> Now, therefore, you are no longer strangers and foreigners, but fellow citizens with the saints and members of the household of God, having been built on the foundation of the apostles and prophets, Jesus Christ Himself being the chief cornerstone. . .

Paul refers to the brethren who worked to spread the gospel as "fellowlabourers" (see Philippians 4:3; Philemon 1:24 KJV). He urged the church in Corinth to accept those whom he sent, not as a bishop leader in the church, but as one who "does the work of the Lord, as I also do" (1 Corinthians 16:10 NKJV). He also refers to Timothy as a "partner and fellowhelper" (2 Corinthians 8:23 KJV).

It is not the preacher standing behind the pulpit who is infallible, but rather the Word of God that is preached. The benchmark for everything done in the church was and is to be the Scriptures. Luke wrote in Acts 17:11–12 of Paul and Silas being sent to Berea. There they found a group eager to hear the message:

> These were more fair-minded than those in Thessalonica, in that they received the word with all readiness, and *searched the Scriptures daily to find out whether these things were so.* Therefore many of them believed. . . . (NKJV, emphasis mine)

Those men and women believed, not because Paul and Silas were infallible, not because the two men co-pastored the most impressive congregation in town, not because they were persuasive speakers, but because the *Word* confirmed their discourse.

S. Michael Houdmann with GotQuestions.org answers the question, "Was Peter the first pope?"

The answer, according to Scripture, is

a clear and emphatic "no." Peter nowhere claims supremacy over the other apostles. Nowhere in his writings (1 and 2 Peter) did the Apostle Peter claim any special role, authority, or power over the church. Nowhere in Scripture does Peter, or any other apostle, state that their apostolic authority would be passed on to successors. Yes, the Apostle Peter had a leadership role among the disciples. Yes, Peter played a crucial role in the early spread of the gospel (Acts chapters 1-10). Yes, Peter was the "rock" that Christ predicted he would be (Matthew 16:18). However, these truths about Peter in no way give support to the concept that Peter was the first pope, or that he was the "supreme leader" over the apostles, or that his authority would be passed on to the bishops of Rome. Peter himself points us all to the true Shepherd and Overseer of the church, the Lord Jesus Christ (1 Peter 2:25).[51]

Despite access to the Scriptures, Peter was installed as the reputed head of the church, and it was but a short step to confer that same authority on its leaders. They, too, would be deemed infallible, incapable of error, and subjects of universal worship. Some believe that the statue of St. Peter in the Vatican was a recycled statue of the Roman god Jupiter, complete with a solar disk hovering above his head. It has since been revealed that the statue was created in the thirteenth century by Italian sculptor Arnolfo di Cambio. It is true that emblems of sun worship rife in pagan religions soon infiltrated Christian illustrations, icons, and images. Some theologians believe that the oft-seen halos depicted on images of Christ and Mary were actually symbols of sun worship.

Sun worship was not the only pagan practice to find its way into the early church. The other observances still celebrated in Christian circles today center around Easter and Christmas, and to a lesser degree, Halloween. Discussions regarding these holidays often strike a particularly sensitive target, especially in the twenty-first century when various religions have adopted some of the symbols associated with the holidays. Just how did Roman influences creep into the church?

Early Christians continued to commemorate Passover, but with different symbols as seen in Luke 22:19–20 (NKJV):

And He took bread, gave thanks and broke it, and gave it to them, saying, "This is My body which is given for you; do this in remembrance of Me." Likewise He also took the cup after supper, saying, "This cup is the new covenant in My blood, which is shed for you."

The early church was viewed as a Jewish cult that still observed Passover (Pesach). Constantine determined that the celebration of Easter should not be overshadowed by the Jewish observance of Passover and was adamant about change. Author John Cornwell wrote:

"It is unbecoming that on the holiest of festivals we should follow the customs of the Jews; henceforth let us have nothing in common with this odious people." An accumulation of imperial measures against Jews ensued: special taxes, a ban on new synagogues, the outlawing of intermarriage between Jews and Christians. Persecution flourished in successive imperial reigns.[52]

Constantine's actions at Nicaea were in keeping with the

custom of marrying pagan practices with Christian tenets. Megan McArdle of the *Daily Beast* wrote:

> Our Western Easter traditions incorporate a lot of elements from a bunch of different religious backgrounds. You can't really say that it's just about resurrection, or just about spring, or just about fertility and sex. You can't pick one thread out of a tapestry and say, "Hey, now this particular strand is what this tapestry's really about." It doesn't work that way; very few things in life do.
>
> The fact is that the Ancient Romans were smart when it came to conquering. In their pagan days, they would absorb gods and goddesses from every religion they encountered into their own pantheon; when the Roman Empire became Christian, the Roman Catholic Church continued to do the same thing, in a manner of speaking.[53]

There is only one sure way to firmly contest inaccuracies and become firmly entrenched in truth, and that is through the Word of God. Paul the apostle wrote to Timothy about the importance of the Word:

All Scripture is given by inspiration of God, and is profitable for doctrine, for reproof, for correction, for instruction in righteousness, that the man of God may be complete, thoroughly equipped for every good work. (2 Timothy 3:16–17 NKJV)

Long before Paul saw his first sunrise, King David wrote, "Your word is a lamp to my feet and a light to my path" (Psalm 119:105 NKJV). John, the beloved disciple, wrote, "And you shall know the truth, and the truth shall make you free" (John 8:32 NKJV). The truth of God is always more reliable than the fiction often embraced by the world.

Embracing pagan practices netted a plethora of new churchgoers, ones not particularly familiar with the ancient texts of the Old Testament. It was, therefore, quite effortless to mix the Easter bunny and brightly decorated eggs of pagan fertility rites in with the solemn remembrance of the death and resurrection of Christ. The story is told of two women searching for an Easter card to send to a friend. One said to the other, "It would be easy to find a card if it weren't for all this religious stuff." Sadly, both Christmas and Easter have become more about secular traditions than about our Lord.

Near the end of each year, the Romans celebrated the

winter solstice within several days of December 22 (when the sun is at its greatest distance from the equator). On that day, Saturnalia—the festival of Saturnus (Roman god of farming)—was celebrated in recognition of the end of agricultural endeavors for the year. Business transactions were halted; courts were shuttered; war was forbidden; and criminals could not be punished. According to *A Dictionary of Greek and Roman Antiquities*, "Many of the peculiar customs exhibited a remarkable resemblance to the sports of our own Christmas and of the Italian Carnival."[54] A tree was decorated with ornaments and *oscilla* (carnival masks) suspended from its branches. Lest you think this was germane to ancient Rome, the majority of pagan cultures embraced customs that are today considered representative of Christmas.

An interesting side note is a passage from the prophet Jeremiah:

> This is what the LORD says:
>
> Do not learn the way of the nations or be terrified by signs in the heavens, although the nations are terrified by them, for the customs of the peoples are worthless. Someone cuts down a tree from the forest; it is worked by the hands of a craftsman with a chisel. He

decorates it with silver and gold. It is fastened
with hammer and nails, so it won't totter.
(Jeremiah 10:2–4 HCSB)

You may ask, "Isn't gift-giving associated with the
arrival of the Magi after the birth of Christ?" The Wise
Men from the East did present gifts, but not because it was
Jesus' birthday; they were welcoming a king. The *Adam
Clarke Commentary* records: "The people of the east never
approach the presence of kings and great personages, without
a present in their hands."[55] Thus, the gifts were not to mark
His birthday, but His Kingship. Gold was a representation
of divinity; frankincense was one of the ingredients of the
special incense burned in the temple during worship; myrrh,
used in the embalming process, was indicative of enmity,
travail, and grief. As Isaiah wrote of the suffering Savior,
"Surely He has borne our griefs and carried our sorrows"
(Isaiah 53:4a NKJV).

The actual date of the birth of Jesus is not specifically
noted in the Bible. With careful study, however, it can be
pinpointed. Dr. David R. Reagan, Lamb and Lion Ministries,
provided insight when he wrote:

> According to Luke 1:24-26, Mary con-
> ceived Jesus in the sixth month of Elizabeth's

pregnancy with John the Baptist. This means that Jesus was born 15 months after the angel Gabriel appeared to Elizabeth's husband, Zacharias, and informed him that his wife would bear a child.

According to Luke 1:5, Zacharias was a priest of the division of Abijah. Luke 1:8 says that Gabriel appeared to Zacharias while he was serving as a priest in the Temple.

We know from the Talmud and other sources that the division of Abijah served as priests during the second half of the fourth month of the Jewish religious calendar—which would have put it in late June (the Jewish religious calendar begins in March with Passover).

Fifteen months later would place the birth of Jesus in the seventh month of the Jewish calendar. That would be in the fall of the year, in either late September or early October. His *conception*, not His birth, would have occurred in December of the previous year.[56] (Emphasis mine.)

Only once in the New Testament are believers instructed to do something in remembrance, and it was not His birth, death, or resurrection. In Luke 22:17–19 (ESV), we read:

> And he took a cup, and when he had given thanks he said, "Take this, and divide it among yourselves. For I tell you that from now on I will not drink of the fruit of the vine until the kingdom of God comes." And he took bread, and when he had given thanks, he broke it and gave it to them, saying, "This is my body, which is given for you. Do this in remembrance of me."

Pastor J.D. Shaw of Grace Bible Church alerted his congregation to the importance of Communion. He said:

> In so many Protestant churches today the Lord's Supper is this optional extra, this add-on, to a worship service. It's an afterthought—*what's really important is the sermon and the music, but then, oh my goodness, it's time for the Lord's Supper again—you know, it's been a month or three months since we last took it, so we'd better squeeze it in Sunday somehow.* We

tend to rush through it, to get it done as some kind of ritual that's not really important but Jesus said we have to do it anyway. That's a very, very low view of the Lord's Supper, and I don't think that's a proper understanding of "remember" either.[57] (Emphasis mine.)

What are we to remember? We are to remember Him, remember the purpose of His birth, the reason for His death, and the promise of His resurrection. Jesus was born to die; He died so that you and I might have our sins forgiven; and He rose from the dead to enable forgiven men and women to spend eternity with Him. This is what we are to "remember."

CONSTANTINE CHANGES CHURCH CUSTOMS

LIVES OF BELIEVERS in Rome changed under Constantine—and not always for the better. Dilution of church precepts and policies following the Nicene Creed created an assembly that was vastly different from that of early Christians. After the changes for Christmas and Easter, there were other major changes:

- ✧ The Sabbath was moved to Sunday.

- ✧ The relationship between Church and State was reclassified.

- ✧ The Temple of Venus became the Church of the Holy Sepulcher.

✧ The blood of Jesus and salvation through grace was redefined as salvation by water baptism.

Roman citizens worshiped a pantheon of gods that included Jupiter, Mars, Venus, Juno, Minerva, Neptune, Ceres, Vulcan, Diana, Bacchus, Mercury, Vesta, and later such gods as Isis, Pan, and Mithras were imported. Added to this group was emperor worship. The deification of an emperor was celebrated throughout the empire. This likely emerged as simple gratitude for the stability afforded by local Roman occupation. Usually, divinity was bestowed upon the death of an emperor and a temple was built in his honor. Julius Caesar was venerated soon after his death in 44 BC. After a time, the sense of appreciation faded and worship of emperors became proof of allegiance to the period's current leader of the empire. Such "hero worship" could be dangerous to the one demanding homage—as we see in Acts 12:

On an appointed day Herod put on his royal robes, took his seat upon the throne, and delivered an oration to them. And the people were shouting, "The voice of a god, and not of a man!" Immediately an angel of the Lord struck him down, because he did not give God the glory, and he was eaten by worms and breathed his last. (Acts 12:21–23 ESV)

What Herod had not understood was Exodus 20:3, which clearly states, "You shall have no other gods before me" (ESV). Herod's presumption of divine status, and the perks that must surely follow, was his downfall.

The refusal of Christians to bow down to the emperor or his envoy was tantamount to a death sentence. According to Oxford Biblical Studies Online:

> Failure to give divine honours to the emperor or 'to swear by the genius of Caesar' was not the only ground for persecution; but the anti-Christian writer Celsus (about 178 CE) warned Christians of the perils of their lack of civic sense and of their disloyalty to an empire from which they derived many material benefits.[58]

After the council at Nicaea, church leaders eased the restrictions on its members with regard to pagan practices. The Catholic Encyclopedia offers this explanation:

> The Church tolerated the cult of the emperor under many forms. It was permitted

to speak of the divinity of the emperor, of the sacred palace, the sacred chamber, and of the altar of the emperor, without being considered on this account an idolater. From this point of view Constantine's religious change was relatively trifling; it consisted of little more than the renunciation of a formality. For what his predecessors had aimed to attain by the use of all their authority, and at the cost of incessant bloodshed, was in truth only the recognition of their own divinity; Constantine gained this end, though he renounced the offering of sacrifices to himself. *Some bishops, blinded by the splendor of the court, even went so far as to laud the emperor as an angel of God, as a sacred being, and to prophesy that he would, like the Son of God, reign in heaven.* It has consequently been asserted that Constantine favored Christianity merely from political motives, and he has been regarded as an enlightened despot who made use of religion only to advance his policy.[59] (Emphasis mine.)

It was persecution that drove the church from the

confines of Jerusalem, Judea, and Samaria and into the "uttermost parts of the earth." As long as the attack had come from without, the followers of Christ were driven together as a unified body of believers. Under Constantine, Satan changed his tactics, sneaking subtly into the very heart of the church and began to attack from within its walls. At the Council of Nicaea, some historians believe the emperor assumed the role of *Summus Pontifex,* or Supreme Pontiff, simply because it was Constantine who called together the bishops for the conference. It was under his leadership that the Church of Rome was formulated.

Knowing that various groups of Christians had made the change from worshiping on Saturday to Sunday as a means to escape persecution, the emperor determined to unite the various groups under a national "Sunday law" enacted in AD 321. In order to divert the church from the pagan practice of gathering to venerate the sun on the first day of the week, fourth-century Christians labeled it the Lord's Day, to little avail. It soon became known worldwide as Sunday. Thus the practice of keeping the Sabbath was lost to all, except the Jews and a few denominations that still today observe Saturday worship.

While those shrewd changes were cleverly interwoven into Christianity, they made the lives of Jews scattered throughout the Roman world a bit of hell on earth. As followers of Christ were spared oppression and persecution, Jews became the target of hateful men with a satanic agenda.

By the time Constantine assumed the throne, Christianity was widespread and, for the most part, at least tolerated. The fly in the ointment was that its followers adamantly refused to worship the emperor. It seems that the wily emperor understood the opportunity before him: The church might actually be the means to restore the feeling of unity in the Roman Empire that had been enjoyed under the first-century rule of Augustus Caesar. Constantine discovered that his intuition was accurate; all he needed to do was bring together the various religious leaders in Rome, Syria, Alexandria, Egypt, and in Antioch. Although language was a barrier and corruption was rampant, he made progress. The result was to bring the church under the rule of the state.

The emperor, who had appointed himself as a bishop, established synods answerable only to him. He, Constantine, would be the one responsible for determining how Christianity might ultimately appear. The changes introduced had a two-fold purpose: church hierarchy could tap state resources to maintain clerical control; and Constantine could manipulate the bishops to suit his own purpose. As a bishop and also the emperor, his word was law at both Church and State levels.

Unlike the early church, which set itself apart from the religious practices of its Roman oppressors, Constantine's new Roman Church was founded to meet the needs of the emperor and thus expand the empire. Orthodoxy ruled in the Church of Rome. Peter Nathan with Vision.org wrote of the meaning of orthodoxy and its impact on the early church:

> The word *orthodoxy* comes from Greek and means literally "to have the right opinion," indicating intellectual agreement. It demands that a person agree, not that he or she behave accordingly. For religion, the result was the development of creeds—authoritative statements to be memorized and used as strict standards of belief by which a certain uniformity could be established. Under this system, whether a person understood underlying concepts was immaterial. Because orthodoxy is a matter of thought and knowledge rather than behavior, it is primarily concerned with philosophy, and it relegates behavior to a secondary position.[60]

Jesus had established with His disciples a group based on belief in the fulfillment of prophetic teachings found in the Word of God. His followers were united in the faith of the birth, death, and resurrection of the Messiah. As change gripped the church, the concept of salvation through grace was replaced by the idea that spiritual rebirth could be gained via water baptism. Some theologians espouse the theory that although Constantine claimed a conversion experience, he waited until he was on his deathbed to be baptized. The apostle Paul wrote to the Church of Rome regarding salvation:

> If you confess with your mouth, "Jesus is Lord," and believe in your heart that God raised Him from the dead, you will be saved. One believes with the heart, resulting in righteousness, and one confesses with the mouth, resulting in salvation. Now the Scripture says, Everyone who believes on Him will not be put to shame, for there is no distinction between Jew and Greek, since the same Lord of all is rich to all who call on Him. For everyone who calls on the name of the Lord will be saved. (Romans 10:9–13 HCSB)

Christian author and pastor Jack Wellman succinctly refuted this belief:

> ... to suggest that being baptized is necessary to being saved is tantamount to saying that Jesus' perfect life, sacrifice, death, and resurrection was not enough: I must add baptism to it to complete the saving work of Christ.[61]

Author and sociology professor Morrie Schwartz stated, "Everything that gets born dies," and on May 22, 337, Constantine was no exception as he followed his ancestors in death. His various heirs fought for years to elevate themselves to a role of leadership, and finally his son Constantius won the battle. His reign was followed by that of Julian, the nephew of Constantine.

Unlike his uncle who had supported Christianity, Julian championed the Jews. On his way to Persia, he inquired of a Jewish legation in Antioch why they no longer offered sacrifices. The answer: It was not permitted. They asked that the temple and altar be rebuilt in Jerusalem. Montifiore relates that Julian "reversed the Hadrianic and Constantinian persecutions, restored Jerusalem to the Jews, returned their property, revoked the anti-Jewish taxes and granted power of taxation and the title Praetorian Prefect to their patriarch Hillel."[62] He also restored the pagan practice of sun worship.

Julian died in an ill-fated attempt to invade Persia. On May 27, 363, Jerusalem suffered an earthquake and the loss of all the materials that had been amassed to rebuild the temple. On June 26, while engaged in a clash near Samarra, Julian was fatally wounded when a spear pierced his liver and intestines. He was succeeded by Jovian, a general in attendance at the time of death. He overturned Julian's acts, banning the Jews from Jerusalem and declaring one truth—that of Jesus Christ. In 391, Theodosius I officially made Christianity the authorized religion of the Roman Empire, and it was he who enforced that edict.

As the fourth century came to a close, the tenets of the early church and its ties to Judaism had been replaced by the politics of the Roman Empire and the belief that anything which interfered with the State religion, anything deemed unorthodox, must be expunged. Sadly, in that new inter-pretation of the church, Jews were unorthodox and must be eradicated. As the Church of Rome gained power, anti-Semitism grew. Even in the fourth century, there remained many Christians with ties to the early church who continued to attend synagogue and observe Jewish holy days, rather than succumb to the modernization policies instituted by Constantine. They, too, began to experience renewed persecution, as did the Jews under Rome's control.

Perhaps Raul Hillberg, Holocaust expert, wrote most convincingly of the trials and tribulation that awaited the Jews from the time of Constantine's conversion:

> Since the fourth century after Christ there have been three anti-Jewish policies: [forced] conversion, expulsion, annihilation. The second appeared as an alternative to the first, and the third emerged as an alternative to the second. . . . The missionaries of Christianity had said in effect: You have no right to live among us as Jews. The secular rulers who followed proclaimed: You have no right to live among us. The Nazis at last decreed: You have no right to live.[63]

ANTI-SEMITISM PROLIFERATES

IF BUT ONE PERSON were to bear accountability in the fourth century for the proliferation of what would in 1879 become known as anti-Semitism, it would be St. John of Chrysostom. Catholic theologian John Henry Cardinal Newman offered the following description of John:

> He was "a bright, cheerful, gentle soul; a sensitive heart, a temperament open to emotion and impulse; and all this elevated, refined, transformed by the touch of heaven,—such was St. John Chrysostom; winning followers, riveting affections, by his sweetness, frankness, and neglect of self."[64]

Unfortunately, this description was applicable only with the church; his compassion, kindheartedness, and understanding were totally lost on the Jewish people. The rabid anti-Semitism practiced by the highly visible church father was put forth in his set of homilies "Against the Jews." In his 1934 book, author James Parkes wrote of Chrysostom:

> Such was the man who in eight sermons covering more than a hundred pages of closely printed text, has left us the most complete monument of the public expression of the Christian attitude to the Jews in the century of the victory of the Church. In these discourses there is no sneer too mean, no gibe too bitter for him to fling at the Jewish people. No text is too remote to be able to be twisted to their confusion, no argument is too casuistical, no blasphemy too startling for him to employ; and, most astonishing of all, at the end he turns to the Christians, and in words full of sympathy and toleration he urges them not to be too hard on those who have erred in following Jewish practices or in visiting Jewish synagogues. Dealing with

the Christians, no text which urges forgiveness is forgotten: dealing with the Jews only one verse of the New Testament is omitted: 'Father, forgive them, for they know not what they do'.

The only explanation of his bitterness contained in the sermons themselves is the too close fellowship between Jews and Christians in Antioch. There is no single suggestion that the Jews were immoral or vicious; no suggestion that Christians were actually corrupted by the contact, either in their morals or their orthodoxy.[65]

It was about that time that the accusation "Christ killers" began to be heard, and the denigration of the Jews by the Church of Rome was sealed. According to Chrysostom, "The Jews have assassinated the Son of God! How dare you [the Church] associate . . . with this nation of assassins and hangmen."[66]

In his first homily on the Jews, St. John Chrysostom wrote vengefully:

I said that the synagogue is no better than a theater and I bring forward a prophet as my witness. Surely the Jews are not more deserving of belief than their prophets. "You had a harlot's brow; you became shameless before all". Where a harlot has set herself up, that place is a brothel. But the synagogue is not only a brothel and a theater; it also is a den of robbers and a lodging for wild beasts. Jeremiah said: "Your house has become for me the den of a hyena". He does not simply say "of wild beast", but "of a filthy wild beast", and again: "I have abandoned my house, I have cast off my inheritance". But when God forsakes a people, what hope of salvation is left? When God forsakes a place, that place becomes the dwelling of demons.[67]

Chrysostom, sometimes referred to as the "patron saint of preachers" delivered sermons that only stoked the fire of Jew-hatred. Such conflagrations resulted in synagogues being burned, Jews being forced to leave their dwellings, being banned from public office, and suffering even worse treatment.

This discrepancy was quite easily fostered because common men were discouraged, perhaps even forbidden, from reading the Bible. It was a practice in effect until the Protestant Reformation. One man drastically affected by the ban on reading the Scriptures was theologian William Tyndale. Tyndale was skilled in multilingualism and surreptitiously translated the Bible from the original Hebrew, a difficult language to master, into English. According to an associate, Tyndale was "so skilled in eight languages – Hebrew, Greek, Latin, Spanish, French, Italian, English, and German, that whichever he speaks, you might think it his native tongue!"[68]

The Bible translation was subsequently banned by Henry VIII, with Tyndale arrested for heresy and treason. He was incarcerated at the castle of Vilvoorden, where he was held captive in a disgusting environment for more than 500 days. On October 6, 1536, William Tyndale was strangled and his body burned in the prison yard.

This move by the Roman Church ensured that the common man knew only what he was told by the clergy. It also made possible the exclusion and vilification of Jews as "Christ killers," and each Passion play presented to the masses dramatized the role of the Jews in the arrest and crucifixion of Jesus. Was that in itself a ploy to take the focus off the Roman role in the horrifying practice of crucifixion? It was, obviously, a scenario designed to focus attention on the Jews and not on the Roman executioners. Seeds of hatred were planted and the move to persecute Jews became an easy decision.

Those seeds were fed and watered by writings such as the following poem by a thirteenth-century poet. It was quoted in Jeremy Cohen's book *Christ Killers*:

> And when they had stripped off his clothes,
>
> The dirty Jews, the stinking dogs,
>
> They inflicted many wounds on him
>
> With daggers and knives
>
> And then, still in the same place, caused
>
> All of the blood to flow from his body
>
> And collected this blood in a vessel.
>
> They did this
>
> Because with this blood, I know,
>
> They wished to celebrate their sacrament;
>
> For it was their custom, and this is no lie,
>
> To obtain a Christian child every year
>
> young, healthy, and rosy,
>
> This child they put to death
>
> In order to have his blood.[69]

Is it any wonder that the Christian population would leave Easter week sacraments and ceremonies with a renewed vigor to promote violence against Jews? Psychologist and journalist Bernard Starr asked the pointed questions:

> What if [the church] had learned that the term "Jew" appears 202 times in the New Testament and that 82 of those mentions are in the Gospels? What if they discovered that the word "Christian" never appears in the Gospels at all? What would the response have been if churchgoers had heard that when Jesus, who was called rabbi by his followers, was not teaching Torah to multitudes of fellow Jews he was praying and teaching in synagogues? What if they had learned that the term "synagogue" appears 44 times in the Gospels? Would they have been shocked to discover that Jesus and his family attended Jewish religious services in the Temple in Jerusalem every year, as prescribed in the Torah? And if Jesus had rejected Judaism, as many were taught and believed, how would they comprehend Jesus telling the Canaanite woman, "I was sent only to the lost sheep of

Israel" (Matthew 15:24)? Or his instruction to his disciples not to take his teachings to the Gentiles but only to "the lost sheep of the house of Israel" (Matthew 10:5)?[70]

At its zenith the Roman Empire extended from the Atlantic coast of Britain to Northern Africa and from mainland Europe to Mesopotamia. By the end of the fourth century, the majesty of the empire was imperiled by the Visigoths under the leadership of Alaric. In 395, Theodosius I died and the empire was divided between his sons—Arcadius, who ruled the east, and Stilicho, who oversaw the western empire as regent for ten-year-old Honorius. Stilicho's German ancestry placed him in dire straits, as he was charged with treason for supposedly having joined forces with Alaric and was subsequently beheaded.

Alaric's plan was simple: He marched on Rome, and his men surrounded the city until bribed by the Roman senate to depart. He besieged the city again in 409 and was finally successful in capturing Rome in 410—with the help of a group of slaves who had rebelled against the Romans. The city of emperors fell ignominiously to the Visigoths. Dr. Peter Heather, professor of Medieval History at King's College in London, wrote:

A large force of Goths entered Rome by
the Salarian Gate and for three days helped
themselves to the city's wealth. The sources,
without being specific, speak clearly of rape
and pillage. . . . the Goths had a field day. By
the time they left, they had cleaned out many
of the rich senatorial houses as well as all
the temples, and had taken ancient Jewish
treasures that had resided in Rome since the
destruction of Solomon's temple in Jerusalem
over three hundred years before. They also
left with treasure of another sort: Galla Pla-
cidia, sister of the reigning western emperor
Honorius. And arson, too, had been on the
agenda—the area around the Salarian Gate
and the old senate building had been among
the casualties . . . the great imperial capital
had been subjected to a smash-and-grab raid
of epic proportions.[71]

After three long and harrowing days, the invaders
retreated from the city, a rag-tag band of conquerors laden
with loot and captives. Traversing the Appian Way, the troops
ransacked as they retreated toward their destination—North

Africa, where their leader Alaric hoped to establish a settlement. He did not reach his destination, but died along the way and was replaced by his brother-in-law Athaulf. Negotiations with the Romans netted the Visigoths a kingdom in southwest France. They set about conquering the Iberian Peninsula and by the fifth century had fulfilled that vision for domination. By 507, the Visigoths had established a formidable kingdom in Gaul (the region corresponding to France, Northern Italy, Belgium, the Netherlands, and parts of Germany) and Spain.

Fortunately for the Jewish inhabitants, the invaders had little regard for the various religious creeds over which they ruled.[72] That changed when Alaric II came to power and summarily espoused the edicts of the conquered Romans.[73] When Visigoth ruler Recared followed Roman custom and embraced Catholicism in the late sixth century, an antagonistic plan regarding treatment of the Jews was promptly enacted.

Under Recared's leadership, the Third Council of Toledo adopted a law requiring children of mixed marriages to be baptized, including offspring of unions between Christians and Jews. Christian women were forbidden to have intercourse with Jewish men—even husbands with wives—and circumcision was banned. The action did not meet with overwhelming success, as not all Visigoths had converted to Catholicism and were, therefore, more lenient toward their Jewish neighbors. The reprieve was not to last forever.

In 612 a new ruler, Sisebut, took the reins of power on the peninsula, and resurrected Recared's program with rekindled energy. Not only did he reinforce the earlier edict of mandatory baptism for children of multicultural unions, Sisebut launched the first proclamation of conversion or expulsion against the Jews. It is thought that nearly 100,000 became *conversos* (new Christians), while some fled the country for the region of Gaul with others going to North Africa. According to author Yom Tov Assis, many of the supposed converts continued to practice Judaism in secret.[74] For many Jews, the "conversions" lasted only until the more lenient reign of Sisebut's successor, Swintila, when many of the conversos reverted to Judaism.

The Fourth Council of Toledo voted to eliminate the practice of compulsory baptism for children of mixed marriages, but added that if a converso was in actuality a practicing Jew, any offspring would be taken from the parents and enrolled in a monastery or entrusted to the household of a confirmed Christian. In this way, all Jews who had reverted to Judaism under the rule of Swintila were to be forced to again convert to Christianity.[75]

Each succeeding Council of Toledo seemed to impose even harsher laws governing Jews in the kingdom. The Eighth Council forbade Jews the rites of circumcision and observing Shabbat. Conversos were forced to agree to either burn or stone to death any of their colleagues who reverted to Judaism. According to Katz, anyone regardless of race or religion who enabled the practice of Judaism was penalized one-quarter of their personal property and then excommunicated from the Church.[76] Through the years and Councils the fate of Jews rose and fell with various rulers—some inclined to relax the punishment of the Jews for perceived wrongdoing, others raising the bar and instituting even more stringent laws.

This disturbing trend instituted under the various Catholic Visigoth rulers was one of growing oppression. So grueling were the demands against Jews that they felt compelled to seek assistance from the Moorish tribes to the south. Charges of conspiring with the enemy were leveled against the Jews and the intolerance only intensified; Jews were subjugated and their property seized.[77]

The Seventeenth Council of Toledo in 694 under Egica decreed:

As the Jews have added to their other crimes this that they endeavoured to overthrow the country and the people, they must be severely punished. They have done this after they had (in appearance) received baptism, which, however, by faithlessness they have again stained. They shall be deprived of their property for the benefit of the exchequer, and shall be made slaves forever. Those to whom the King sends them as slaves must watch that they may no longer practise Jewish usages, and their children must be separated from them, when they are seven years of age, and subsequently married with Christians.[78]

Under various edicts issued by the Church and/or rulers in Spain, a Christian woman, married or single, daughter or prostitute, was forbidden to enter the home of a Jew. A woman who broke this law had to forfeit the dress she was wearing; a married woman was required to pay a fine of four hundred *maravedis* (a gold or silver Spanish coin); and a prostitute faced one hundred lashes and expulsion from her place of lodging. A Jew who was intimate with a

Christian woman, even if it was his wife, faced being burned
at the stake.

The Muslim invasion under Tariq ibn Ziyad vividly
changed the lives of Spanish Jews on the Iberian Peninsula.
Historians of the time recount the beneficial aid provided
to the Moors by the Jews.[79] Having been totally disillu-
sioned and estranged by the edicts handed down by the
Catholic Church, the Jews saw the Moors as an emanci-
pating force and chose to help the invaders.[80] The period
of Muslim rule on the Iberian Peninsula came to be known
as the Golden Age by the Sephardic Jews who settled in
the area.

In *The Origins of the Inquisition*, Benzion Netanyahu
wrote:

> The Moorish-Arab conquest of the Iberian
> Peninsula in 711–714, ended the first cycle
> of Jewish life in Christian Spain. In the iso-
> lated spots of northern Spain that remained
> under Christian control, no Jews lived after
> 714; nor did Jews live in any of the territories
> "reconquered" by the Spaniards in the course
> of the eighth and the early ninth centuries.
> Those who did not flee southward to the

Muslims were killed by Christian raiders or conquerors.[81]

The Iberian Peninsula was, for Muslims, Christians, and Jews, a bit of paradise. The region was separated from the barbarism of Europe by the rugged Pyrenees Mountains. The peoples of the various regions encapsulated on the peninsula each supported the other in this period labeled *convivencia*—or coexistence. The three groups lived "in amity, respecting differences while honoring commonalities."[82] In Cordoba, for instance, Christians worshiped in the Great Mosque, something unheard of today. Muslim teachers schooled Jews in Arabic and in the Quran, as well as astronomy, mathematics, and medicine. Conversely, Jews taught Christians in such regions as Castile and Catalonia.

MURDER AND MAYHEM

THIS TRANQUIL STATE of coexistence and cooperation extended into the eleventh century when the services and expertise of Jewish and Christian professionals, including doctors, astronomers, and scientists, were highly sought and esteemed. One Jew who served as vizier under King Habbus in Granada, one of the independent Muslim-governed principalities, was Samuel Ha-Nagid ibn Nagrela. So respected was he that both Nagrela and his son Joseph served as military leaders of a Muslim army.

The Jewish Virtual Library relates the details of the Granada massacre of 1066:

> When Jews were perceived as having achieved too comfortable a position in Islamic

society, anti-Semitism would surface, often
with devastating results: On December 30,
1066, Joseph HaNagid, the Jewish vizier of
Granada, Spain, was crucified by an Arab mob
that proceeded to raze the Jewish quarter of
the city and slaughter its 5,000 inhabitants.
The riot was incited by Muslim preachers
who had angrily objected to what they saw
as inordinate Jewish political power.[83]

The assault against Jews in Granada was an early indication that their status was changing—and not for the better. Between 1095 and 1099, the Crusaders, under the direction of Pope Urban II, descended on Jerusalem and its Jewish inhabitants in several attempts to retake the Holy Land. What began as a series of pilgrimages soon became an armed expedition to reclaim the Holy City from the marauding Seljuk Turks, thereby liberating Christians from Muslim rule.

The first Crusade degenerated into a cumbersome contrivance comprised of the grander nobles and less significant counterparts, i.e. Count Emicho (a.k.a. Emich) of Leiningen. They were joined by a dubious horde of undesirables who swelled the ranks but possessed no military discipline. This group was easily aroused to a frenzied pitch and then turned loose to wreak mayhem as they made their way toward Jerusalem. An anti-Jewish slogan tossed into their midst would end in a murderous riot, with Jews being the target. Those nobles in charge of the procession, while outwardly opposed to the attacks, did little to halt the ensuing bedlam.

Jews along the route were subjected to violence during the celebration of Passover and Shavout. In May 1096, Crusaders encircled the synagogue in Speyer but were unsuccessful in their attempt to gain entry. They turned their attention to any hapless Jew who might be on the streets of the city. Three weeks later, Jews in the city of Worms suffered the same fate. First to be slaughtered were approximately 800 Jews who chose to remain in their homes.

When a band of Crusaders, under the leadership of Count Emicho, reached the outskirts of the city, the remaining Jews took refuge in the palace of the bishop. He, too, was forced to flee the onslaught of the unruly pilgrims. Author Deanna Proach wrote of Count Emicho's assault:

> Emich and his men set fire to the bishop's palace and slaughtered Jews mercilessly, sparing no man, woman and child, except perhaps those who decided to renounce their faith. Those who were spared killed

themselves to avoid any potential suffering. "The women slaughtered their sons
and daughters, then themselves. Many of
the men too, slaughtered their wives, their
sons and children," the Jewish chronicler,
Saloman bar Simson wrote. "One man burnt
down the synagogue to keep it from further
desecration, then killed himself and his
family."

About 1,000 Jews were slaughtered in the
Mainz massacre, enough for the merciless
Emich to consider his work in the Rhineland
done. He set out east for the Holy Land, but
a large part of his army broke off and headed
into the Moselle Valley where they ravaged
more Jewish colonies.[84]

The bloodbath continued in Cologne, Trier, and other
villages along the route. In the town of Regensburg, Jewish
residents were hauled down to the Danube and forcefully
baptized. It did little good, as carnage followed massacre
and brutal butchery claimed countless lives. The end did
not come until Emicho was immobilized by the Hungarians,
who were enraged by the ruthlessness that had gripped their

country. When the atrocities ceased, more than 5,000 Jews had died at the hands of the Crusaders.

The summer of 1099 found 1,200 knights and 21,000 soldiers surrounding the walls of Jerusalem. Montefiore describes the challenges the Crusaders faced once near the Holy City:

> ... their Western horses had long since perished or been eaten by the hungry army. In the blistered gorges around Jerusalem, charges were impossible, horses useless and armour too hot: this exhausted force of Franks had to fight on foot, while their leaders feuded constantly. There was no supreme commander. Pre-eminent among them, and also the riches, was Raymond, Count of Toulouse. A courageous but uninspiring leader, noted for obstinacy and lack of tact ... The princes were already bickering over the spoils. . . . The heat was unforgiving, the sirocco blew, water was short, men too few, morale low, and the Egyptians were approaching. There was no time to lose. . . . By night on 13 July, the Crusaders were ready.[85]

And so, the bloody battle began. The Crusaders under the leadership of men such as Raymond, Godfrey of Bouillon, the Duke of Normandy and Count of Flanders, Tancred de Hauteville, and the Duke of Lower Lorraine stormed the walls of the fortified city. After breaching the walls, the slaughter began. No one was safe. Anyone in the path of the Crusaders was murdered; hands, feet, and heads were severed from bodies. Children were torn from the arms of their mothers and bashed against the stone walls of the city. Montefiore records the eyewitness account of Raymond of Aguilers:

> Wonderful sights were to be seen. Our men cut off the heads of their enemies, others tortured them longer by casting them into the flames. Piles of heads, hands and feet were to be seen on the streets. It was necessary to pick one's way over the bodies of men and horses.[86]

Synagogues were torched, killing all those who had taken refuge inside. No one escaped the brutality—man, woman, or child. On the Temple Mount alone more than 10,000 were massacred. The streets of Jerusalem were strewn with the body parts of the slain. The stench of rotting flesh under the hot Middle Eastern sun was overwhelming. Such ruthlessness was the legacy of a "holy war." When the violence had ended, there were scarcely enough inhabitants to fill even one-quarter of the city. The solution was to wage war on Jordan and invite Syrian and Armenian Christians to settle in Jerusalem. They were the ancestors of today's Palestinian Christians.

Seven major crusades, as well as unnumbered smaller excursions to the Holy Land, followed the first. During the initial foray to retake Jerusalem, the Europeans managed to secure a small strip of land that extended from Antioch in Turkey to Jerusalem. That expanse was given the designation of "Jerusalem." When the area was later endangered, St. Bernard of Clairvaux, a French abbot, accompanied by German and French forces began a second crusade. The army turned aside to strike Damascus but was defeated in battle.

The third crusade began when King Richard the Lionheart of England joined with two other kings, Frederick Barbarossa of Germany and Philip Augustus of France, in an attempt to liberate Jerusalem from Saladin, its Muslim captor. After Frederick drowned and Philip decided to return to France, Richard was successful only in reaching an agreement with Saladin that allowed Christian pilgrims access to Jerusalem.

Other attempts to regain the Holy City were largely failures. The Crusaders that gathered in 1202 failed to reach the Middle East, instead attacking Constantinople and establishing a Latin empire in that great city. Jerusalem was all but forgotten. Although the fervor of the Crusaders did little to help them achieve their original goal, it did have substantial consequences: The ideal of and respect for the papal leaders in Europe was diminished. The word *crusade* came to have a dark meaning for many in the Near and Middle East due to the actions of the various leaders.

Thomas F. Madden, associate professor and chair of the Department of History at Saint Louis University, wrote of the unifying purpose of the Crusades:

> By the eighth century, Muslim armies had conquered all of Christian North Africa and Spain. In the eleventh century, the Seljuk Turks conquered Asia Minor (modern Turkey), which had been Christian since the time of St. Paul. The old Roman Empire, known to modern historians as the Byzantine Empire, was reduced to little more than Greece. In desperation, the emperor in Constantinople sent word to the Christians

of western Europe asking them to aid their brothers and sisters in the East.

That is what gave birth to the Crusades. They were not the brainchild of an ambitious pope or rapacious knights but a response to more than four centuries of conquests in which Muslims had already captured two-thirds of the old Christian world. At some point, Christianity as a faith and a culture had to defend itself or be subsumed by Islam. The Crusades were that defense. . . .

Whether we admire the Crusaders or not, it is a fact that the world we know today would not exist without their efforts. The ancient faith of Christianity, with its respect for women and antipathy toward slavery, not only survived but flourished. Without the Crusades, it might well have followed Zoro-astrianism, another of Islam's rivals, into extinction.[87]

Even as Crusaders were attempting to reclaim Jeru-salem, Jews in Europe were undergoing harsh, and some-times deadly, persecution.

TRIALS AND TERRORS

AS ARMOR was being polished and horses festooned with ribbons and banners, plans were being made for another crusade into Muslim-held Jerusalem. Several kings from Europe issued edicts that caused great pain and suffering to Jews living under their control. Author Edward Flannery wrote of those devastating times:

> To find a year more fateful in the history of Judaism than 1096 would necessitate going back a thousand years to the fall of Jerusalem or forward to the genocide of Hitler. Though often surpassed by other years in the volume of atrocities, 1096 marks the beginning of a harassment of the Jews that, in duration and

intensity, was unique in Jewish history. . . .
There were mutterings that the Crusaders might better start their work with the
"infidels at home." One chronicler, Gilbert
of Nogent (1053–1124) reported the Crusaders of Rouen as saying: "We desire to combat
the enemies of God in the East; but we have
under our eyes the Jews a race more inimical
to God than all the others. We are doing this
whole thing backwards." Turning this logic
into action, the Crusaders fell upon the Jews
in Rouen and other places in Lorraine, mas-
sacring those who refused baptism.[88]

All too often, persecution and murder followed a revival
of the "blood libel" lie that had been attached to Jews. Some
historians believe it originated in the twelfth century when
a young tanner's apprentice, William of Norwich, was said
to have been abducted and ritually murdered by Jews in
his town. William was later found having been stabbed to
death. A Jew was slaughtered in retaliation on Good Friday.
A Benedictine monk, Thomas of Monmouth, penned an
account of the child's death that many believe is the origin of
the fictional tale regarding "blood libel." And so, a falsehood

JEW-HATRED AND THE CHURCH

was established as fact. Thomas claimed that each year a group of Jews gathered to determine from what country a child would be taken and sacrificed during the Easter season. It was his contention that England was the locale chosen in 1144, with William the legendary victim. This bit of fiction was all that was needed to inflame anti-Semites in England, France, Germany, and eventually other European countries. The claim of blood libel was a virus that was incubated in the Church, fueled by the Crusaders, and spewed forth wherever anti-Semitism reigned.

Rabbi and Professor Marc Saperstein commented on this phenomenon in his book *Moments of Crisis in Jewish-Christian Relations*:

> "Thus the earliest recorded account of Jewish ritual murder . . . is embellished with the suggestion of an international Jewish conspiracy, and sanctioned by ancient Jewish texts, which Christians ought to fear. . . . A chilling conclusion is placed by the author in the mouths of the 'populace' which cried out 'with one voice that all the Jews ought to be utterly destroyed as constant enemies of the Christian name and the Christian religion.'

Such a sentence indicated that a 'Final Solution' was at least conceivable in the Middle Ages."[89]

In 1179 King Philip II Augustus was crowned ruler of France. In need of replenishing the coffers, he targeted the rich—namely Jews. Philip confiscated their wealth and in so doing gained the favor of both the Church and Christians who owed debts to the king's Jewish citizenry. Did the king actually believe the blood libel charges against the Jews, or was it simply an excellent cover story for his brutal actions against them? Four months later, the king took another step in his assault on the Jews of France: He ordered them all incarcerated and then summarily confiscated their lands. This was soon followed by a demand for ransom, which was paid for their release. In 1181, Philip canceled loans that the Jews had made to French Christians. One year later, the Jews were driven from French territory under his purview.

By 1198, Philip Augustus realized his folly in having the Jews removed from France and allowed them to return. He subsequently taxed their banking practices, developing a lucrative income to line his pockets.

While Philip was ruling in France, Richard the Lionheart had ascended the throne in England. Overt persecution of

Jews under his reign began even during his coronation in 1189. Historian Roger of Hoveden (a.k.a. Howden) detailed events of Richard's ceremony:

> While the king was seated at table, the chief men of the Jews came to offer presents to him, but as they had been forbidden the day before to come to the king's court on the day of the coronation, the common people, with scornful eye and insatiable heart, rushed upon the Jews and stripped them, and then scourging them, cast them forth out of the king's hall. Among these was Benedict, a Jew of York, who, after having been so maltreated and wounded by the Christians that his life was despaired of, was baptised by William, prior of the Church of Saint Mary at York, in the Church of the Innocents, and was named William, and thus escaped the peril of death and the hands of the persecutors.
>
> The citizens of London, on hearing of this, attacked the Jews in the city and burned their houses; but by the kindness of their Christian friends, some few made their escape. On the

day after the coronation, the King sent his servants, and caused those offenders to be arrested who had set fire to the city; not for the sake of the Jews, but on account of the houses and property of the Christians they had burnt and plundered, and he ordered some of them to be hanged.[90]

This event was followed in March 1190 by a massacre of approximately 150 Jews in York. The men, women, and children had taken refuge in Clifford's Tower, part of the royal castle in the city. When attacked by men thirsting for blood, the entire group of Jews either committed suicide to avoid forced baptism or were slaughtered by the rioters who were "without any scruple of Christian conscientiousness."[91]

As a result of decades of manipulation by the kings who ruled England, the Jewish population was often charged with usury and profiteering. English bankers were forbidden by law to practice lending money and charging interest on the funds. The ban did not apply to Jews as their religion, Judaism, did permit the practice. Consequently, Jewish lenders made large sums of money on which the king could levy substantial taxes, and at his leisure withdraw funds.

The monarch needed no approval from any source to tap into that source of revenue.

Unfortunately the Jewish population was accused of extortion by those who had borrowed from them—a charge supported by the Church. It was not long before Jew-hatred was yet again the order of the day. The timeless epithet of "Christ-killers," fueled by myths and gossip reemerged and became widespread—including in Scotland and Wales. Edward I was the English king to adopt the wearing of a yellow badge of shame for Jewish residents. In an edict, the Statute of Jewry, he ordered:

> Each Jew, after he is seven years old, shall wear a distinguishing mark on his outer garment, that is to say, in the form of two tables joined, of yellow felt of the length of six inches and of the breadth of three inches.[92]

The edict also banned the practice of charging interest for money loaned. In 1287, Jews in the Duchy of Gascony were expelled, their holdings confiscated by the king, and any debts owed made payable to the Crown. On July 18, 1289, an Edict of Expulsion was signed, followed by the deportation of 16,000 from the country. Most Jews escaped for a time to France, the Netherlands, and Poland. Between their expulsion and formal invitation to return to England, there is little evidence of a Jewish community in England.

Jews in every city, town, and village soon discovered that the virus of anti-Semitism had no cure. No potion could halt its spread; no elixir would quench its thirst for blood. No technique of torture or dreadful method of death was too vile to be inflicted upon Jews. A brief timeline reveals only a broad overview of the persecutions that took place late in the thirteenth century and through the fourteenth century:

- ✧ **1298**—Persecution of the Jews in Franconia, Bavaria, and Austria. The Nobleman Kalbfleish alleged that he had received a divine order to destroy all the Jews. 140 Jewish communities were destroyed, and more than 100,000 Jews were mercilessly killed.

- ✧ **1306**—King Philip the Fair banished the Jews from France. 100,000 Jews left the country.

- ✧ **1320**—In France, 40,000 shepherds dedicated themselves for the Shepherd Crusade to free Palestine from the Moslems.

Under the influence of criminals and land speculators, they destroyed 120 Jewish communities.

✧ 1321—Jews were accused of having incited outlaws to poison wells and fountains in the district of Guienne, France. . . . 5,000 Jews were burned at the stake.

✧ 1348—Jews were blamed for the plague throughout Europe, especially in Germany. In Strausberg 2,000 Jews were burned. In Maintz 6,000 were killed in [a] most gruesome fashion, and in Erfut 3,000; and in Worms 400 Jews burned themselves in their homes.

✧ 1370—Jews were blamed for having defiled the "Host" (wafer used in the Mass) in Brabant. The accused were burned alive. Again, all Jews were banned from Flanders and until the year 1820, every 15 years a feast was kept to celebrate the event.

✧ 1391—Persecutions in Spain. In Seville and 70 other Jewish communities, the

Jews were cruelly massacred and their bodies dismembered.[93]

It was, perhaps, in Spain that Jews suffered one of the most horrific assaults of early times—the Spanish Inquisition.

THE POGROMS
OF 1391

AS THE FOURTEENTH CENTURY neared an end, another flood of anti-Semitism gripped the region. The fiery preaching of Ferrant Martinez, archdeacon of Ecija, led to a rise in Jew-hatred and the pogroms that often followed. They began in June 1391.

On June 4 of that year, a pogrom against Jews in Seville erupted as riots broke out in the city—something that had not occurred in nearly three hundred years, not since 1109. The Jews, within the *Juderia* (Jewish Quarter) had apparently felt the stirrings of an uprising, for the gates had been closed and closely guarded. A plot to burn down the wooden gates to gain entrance to the area succeeded. Two days later, a horde descended on the Juderia, murdering 4,000 Jews. Those not slaughtered had chosen baptism as the only possible means of evading a death sentence.

In Cordova, the entire Jewish Quarter was burned to the ground with the men, women, and children brutally butchered. When some semblance of calm returned, countless homes and synagogues had been destroyed, the bodies of 2,000 Jews callously piled in the streets. The list of towns and villages where Jewish inhabitants were persecuted, massacred, or forced into Christian baptism grew as the spirit of murder spread across Spain. Toledo, Castilian, Aragon, Majorca, Valencia, and Barcelona, just to name a few cities, were caught up in the frenzy of rioting—and the Jews were the ones to suffer at the hands of hysterical mobs.

Thousands of Jews were wiped from the land, communities obliterated, the perpetrators generally unpunished, and the country suffered from the loss of great minds, gifted artisans, prolific farmers, and productive citizens.

Rabbi Joseph Albo described the scene in Seville during the mob-inspired riots:

A blood-thirsty mob fell on the Jewish quarter of Seville . . . and mercilessly killed every Jew who fell into their hands and refused to be baptized; many women and children were sold into slavery. A number of Jews, however, managed to escape . . . Within three months most of the flourishing Jewish communities in all the Christian States of Spain—Castille, Aragon, Valencia, Catalonia, as well as the Balearic Islands—were destroyed. One of the eye-witnesses to these massacres and atrocities was the famed Rabbi and scholar Hasdai Crescas . . . The pattern was invariably the same: A wild mob, roused by fanatical priests and monks, stormed into the Jewish quarter. They set fire to Jewish homes, shops and synagogues, giving the Jews one choice: conversion to Christianity or death. They killed mercilessly those who refused to be baptized. Many Jews chose to die as martyrs, at *kiddush hashem*[94] [to sanctify His name]; some saved themselves by outward conversion.[95]

When the last drop of Jewish blood had been washed from the streets after the perpetrators of the pogroms had spent their hateful energy, three factions surfaced:

- ✧ Jews who firmly adhered to their faith no matter the cost;

- ✧ Jews who had converted to Christianity and been accepted by the Church;

- ✧ Jews who practiced Christian rituals outwardly, but who were secret Jews still.

Even though conversion seemed to be the solution to those faced with slaughter, the marauding mobs still plundered and burned homes and lands as the Jews awaited baptism. The area was described as resembling a torched wasteland in the wake of the riots. Many Jews were not given the opportunity to convert but were slaughtered with the broadsword, drowned in rivers, burned alive, or sold into slavery. Entire communities disappeared as rioting Jew-haters rushed through towns and villages. It was said that leaders were so frightened by the mob mentality sweeping Spain that they failed to offer any protection against the horror. Sensing the change in attitude, Ferrant Martinez launched a new attack; he described his Jewish adversaries as "incorrigible criminals who attempted to cheat even God himself, and nobody should therefore be surprised that they were cheating the kings and the princes." He reminded them that "Had not Jesus said to his disciples when he sent them to preach the Gospel that anyone who would refuse Jesus' reign should be viewed as His enemy and as son of the devil? Whom does this definition fit more than the Jews, who have consistently rejected His reign. . .?"[96] Martinez demanded that Jews and Christians be separated and that synagogues be dismantled as demanded by decree. While ecclesiastical law prohibited the murder of Jews simply because of their ancestry, he advocated that the multitudes should do exactly that. He assured them immunity from retribution by the powers that be.

Martinez was duly famous for his obstinacy and the tenacity to attain his goals. Discipline, joined with his cruelty and ingenuity as well as his corruptness and determination, made him essentially uncontainable. Due to this amalgamation of abilities he triumphed over the forcefulness of kings, the archbishop of Seville, and the nobility. His celebrity and reputation were enhanced by his rhetoric, which must have been rousing and particularly befitting to move the multitudes. (To comprehend this, we have to search no further back in history than Adolf Hitler.)

It was principally due to sheer eloquence that Martinez captured the fancy of the lower class, which saw him as defender of their Christian cause. The only reason they had held back from inflicting terror on their Jewish neighbors was fear of what the monarchs might do in retaliation. Martinez schooled them in overcoming that fear. He taught them that in terrorizing, and even murdering Jews, they were performing a service to the Crown, not disobeying the laws of the land. His cunning and shrewd activities lasted more than fourteen years as he instigated conflict between the Jews and their countrymen. Had he been given the blessing of the Church and the Crown, it is highly likely that his reign of terror would have eventually encompassed the whole of Spain and all the Jews therein.

Those in charge of the towns and cities failed to suppress the rioters, fearing the mob more than the monarch. For example, in Valencia, some Jews fled but the majority took up crosses, rushed to the cathedrals, and voiced their wish to be baptized. Their conversions led to the total annihilation of the Jewish society in that city. As likely as not, when they returned from awaiting baptism at the local church, they found their homes had been ransacked and personal effects either confiscated or destroyed. Many of the converts lost business partners, either to death or dispersion. These conversos were forced to find and inveigle a Christian to employ them at a vastly lower rate of pay and to work longer hours in order to provide for their families.

Thus Martinez was responsible for inflaming the masses and launching the devastating riots of 1391 that resulted in the butchery of thousands of Jewish men and the conversion of some 20,000 Jews. Such success only intensified the determination of Martinez and his gang of henchmen to further expand their activities across Spain. Only the arrest and incarceration of Martinez's nephew, also a priest, signaled the halt of the pogrom launched by his anti-Semitic uncle.

The attributes of the pogrom of 1391 perhaps describes the vast swarm of conversions that took place in each of the neighborhoods even before the assaults began. The royal edict proposing conversion as an option to death engendered an almost total conversion in many Jewish communities. The riots combined the methods followed by intimidating governments with those of other pogroms and were inflamed by the masses whose purpose was primarily hatred and greed. The result was a sizeable number of converts and a comparably lesser sum of martyrs for the faith.

Jews had been forced to make one of only three choices: expulsion from Spain, conversion to Christianity, or death. Given the reach of the Spanish Inquisition, conversion would eventually mean death for many of the conversos. The forced conversions in Spain during the 1391 riots and pogroms were the precursor to the Inquisition launched under the direction of King Ferdinand and Queen Isabella. The number of Jews who submitted to the coercion of forcible conversion was quite large and included many of the wealthy who ultimately became bitter enemies and oppressors of their Jewish brethren.

Thus the conversos and Marranos became the targets of the inquisitors who would invent and/or endorse the most heinous of acts against the supposed betrayers of the Faith and the Church. The word *Marrano* comes from an Arabic word that means "forbidden, anathematized." In fifteenth-century Spain it came to mean "pig" and "dirty." It was a racist epithet used in a prejudicial way. There have been various explanations as to the etymology of the word, including the Aramaic-Hebrew *Mar Anus* or "forced convert"; and the second word of the religious oath *anathema maranatha* or "cursed at the final judgment." No matter the origin, it was meant to be derisive. *Converso* simply meant to have converted from Judaism to Christianity.

No widespread epidemic hostile to Jews in the Middle Ages produced such staggering loss as did the riots and pogroms of 1391. Jewish fatalities in the Rhineland[97] all through the first Crusade in 1096 or in Germany during the Black Death of 1348[98] were no harsher than those of the Jews in Spain in 1391. If we consider those Jews who abandoned their faith because of intimidation during the riots, the demise of Spain's Jews far outstripped those encountered elsewhere. Within two or three years, Spain's Jewish society, the biggest in the known world, was diminished by almost 33 percent—the utmost calamity that had at that time transpired among Jews in Europe.

DIVISIVE DISUNITY

NEITHER THE MARRANOS nor the conversos were held in especially high esteem by their fellow countrymen. In reality, Spain was boiling with frustration, and the pressure resulting from the addition of all the new converts was taxing the tolerance of the Church and its people. Being forced to convert under duress presented an entirely new set of problems for the conversos. Under constant scrutiny, Jews were forced to forego any semblance of their former lives or rituals, required to work on religious holidays, and banned from working on the Christian Sabbath and festival days. Eventually, Judaic traditions among the conversos declined, while Christian practices blossomed.

Late in the fifteenth century the position of the

aristocracy as well as that of the lower classes changed regarding the conversos. It is believed that they hid their Jewishness beneath a façade of Christianity. By 1449 conversos were banned from holding public office in Toledo no matter how long since their families had converted to Catholicism.[99] This same law presented another concept, that of the *limpieza de sangre*, the "purity of the blood," reminiscent of Nuremberg Laws established by the Nazis in the twentieth century.[100] A division between Old Christians and conversos was created in which conversos were deemed to be subordinate. The newly instituted rule was censured by theologians who determined that all persons who had been baptized into the Church were Christians and should not fall into condemnation.

Suddenly, the Old Christians saw themselves, not the Jewish converts, as the oppressed. Actually, they were no worse off but perceived that they had become socially and economically debased because of their converso neighbors. They felt there was no way to change the government's favorable policies toward the New Christians, thus the anti-Marrano/converso faction would be forced to take the law into their own hands. A steady tide of social, economic, and political advancement among conversos would prove to be the catalyst for the Toledan laws enacted in 1449.

Soon the first flash of hatred as a result of the newly enacted laws against the Marranos arced and would rapidly consume the entire group. It quickly advanced from spark to inferno and launched a new period of struggle between Old Christians and the New in Spain.

The laws signaled the start of an anti-converso movement among the inhabitants of both Castile and Aragon. Hatred of Marranos and conversos flared, as did the violence leveled against them. It was comprised of two parts: 1) a Preamble setting forth a judgment of the social and religious conduct of the conversos; and 2) legal limitations that were to be imposed on them. The law was given a name that reflected the two segments: *Sentencia-Estatuto* (Judgment and Statute).

Chronicler Benzion Netanyahu wrote, "Each of these documents bears witness to the motives, attitudes, doctrines, and convictions that shaped the views of the anti-Marrano party."[101]

The Jewish people were regarded as a problem that could not be resolved by baptism and conversion to Christianity. The statute deprived conversos of the ability to hold any public office or to effectively defend themselves in the courts, and instituted a ban against making a living as clergy in the Church. The laws extended to their descendants in perpetuity. The tenets were designed to strip conversos of all Christian fellowship.

The *Sentencia* (judgment) portion of the document embraced the ideology that conversos filled most public offices in Toledo which dealt with fiscal issues. This, the anti-Marranos exposited, was what allowed them to dominate Old Christians in the entire region. Conspiracy theories against the Jews—both practicing and converts—abounded in Spain in the Middle Ages. The charge required no substantiation; it was enough that those accused had Jewish blood flowing through their veins.

Fingers were pointed at the conversos who managed the king's fiscal administration; they were accused of "having stolen large and innumerable quantities of maravedis (a Moorish gold dinar) and silver from the King our Lord and from his revenues, taxes, and tributes . . . [and] have brought devastation upon the estates of many noble ladies, caballeros and hijos dalgo [little children] . . . [and] have oppressed, destroyed, robbed and deprived most of the old houses and estates of Old Christians of this city, its territory and jurisdiction."[102]

The Toledan Petition, as it came to be known, was the initial manifestation of the anti-Marrano attitude that was prevalent in the country but previously had been officially inhibited. It was the prescribed position adopted by a sector of the people of Spain toward the Marranos and what many considered the Marrano problem. Additionally, it was the initial manifestation of a viewpoint that was to permeate every aspect of Spanish existence. It was a giant step toward the horror that would engulf Spain at the hands of their inquisitors, and a perfect parallel to Psalm 83:3 (ESV): "They lay crafty plans against your people; they consult together against your treasured ones." The conversos were too easy a target for the frequent charges of conspiracy. They were charged with seeking jurisdiction over key court positions by attempting to control and oppress the Old Christians of Spain.

The forces that brought about the launch of the Inquisition were based on religious, socio-economic, and racial factors. In his book on the life of Jewish statesman and philosopher Don Isaac Abravanel, Benzion Netanyahu wrote:

> It was in the year of 1480—the year in which the Cortes of Toledo helped the kings break the powers of the feudal aristocracy— that the Spanish monarchy embarked upon a determined and unrelenting anti-Jewish course. In that year steps were initiated for

the segregation of the Jews and their elimination from Spanish life, and it was in that year that the Inquisition was established. The Inquisition, although directed not against Jews but against Jewish converts and their descendants, was nevertheless the most radical anti-Jewish measure taken at any time in the Middle Ages . . . Spain was the only country in the Middle Ages where Jews were converted to Christianity on a mass scale. . . . The moment a Jew embraced Christianity, all discrimination against him was to end. But this was not the attitude of the burgher. The latter sought, not the Jew's conversion, but rather his annihilation or expulsion.[103]

Even with the institution of the Inquisition and the war against Marranos who had long been converts to Catholicism, Abravanel rebelled against the idea that those tortured and burned at the stake were secret Jews who still practiced the tenets of the faith. Abravanel felt that Marranos, by and large, were traitors to Judaism and had deserted their race to "intermingle" with the Gentiles. He turned to the prophet Hosea 7:8 (NKJV) to support his belief of what had happened to the Marranos: "Ephraim has mixed himself among the peoples; Ephraim is a cake unturned." Abravanel would probably have approved of the *New Living Translation*'s succinct statement: "The people of Israel mingle with godless foreigners, making themselves as worthless as a half-baked cake!"

Abravanel believed that the Marranos had been exposed to the fire—a just punishment for their apostasy. His unrelenting disdain for the Marranos seems a clear indication that many had embraced Catholicism and were true converts, and thus there was no reason for them to be subjected to the terrors of the Inquisition. The charges that they were secret Jews, still practicing the rites of their religion, were unfounded and sprang basically from covetousness. So little credence has been given to the idea that this charge was at the root of the Inquisition, it has been largely unexplored by historians. As Netanyahu indicated:

> The Old Christians thus came to realize the
> fateful mistake they had made when they forced
> the Jews to embrace Christianity, thereby by
> their own hands opening for them the way to
> all the advantages and positions which they had
> so vehemently fought to deny them.[104]

The general consensus is that the Marranos were, indeed, Christians, and not Jews covertly clinging to Judaism. It is inordinately sad that the Old Christians resented the Marranos for having embraced the very religion they were forced to accept upon threat of death. Can we then assume that the Marranos might very well have been singled out for the same reason so many of Israel's children are so unpopular today? They are Jews—the offspring of Abraham, Isaac, and Jacob. They are the children of the covenant between God and His people.

Centuries before the term "Nazism" was introduced into the language, there were racists. Long before Hitler's troops goose-stepped through the capitals of Europe, anti-Semitism reigned supreme. Years before the Jews were charged with creating the chaos that was Germany's economic upheaval, Jew-hatred permeated that society. Holocaust historian Raul Hilberg wrote, "The Nazis did not discard the past, they built on it. They did not begin a development. They completed it."[105]

It did not even begin in Spain in the Middle Ages. It began when the children of Israel resolved to be a distinctive group of people, set apart by their faith in one God (Jehovah) and by the denunciation of the predominant religion of the day. They, then, all too often were charged with being the culprits, real or imagined, for whatever adversities were visited upon the world. The anti-Semites down through the ages might well have quoted author Andrew Bernaldez: "Once the fire has been ignited, it will be necessary for it to go on burning until all the Judaizers are consumed and dead, and none of them remains."[106]

According to the Southern Institute for Education and Research at Tulane University in New Orleans, Louisiana:

In the late 19th century, the debate on the Jewish question entered a new chapter. Hitherto, the Jews had been viewed as different and unacceptable because of their religion. In 1873, with the publication of the book *The Victory of Judaism over Germanism* by Wilhelm Marr, the Jewish question became one of race. The Jews, it was argued, were different because of who they were, not what they thought. They were different because of birth. They were different because of blood. An "alien" people, the Jews could never be Germans. It was in this book that the term anti-Semitism first appeared. This so-called scientific basis of anti-Semitism excluded any possibility of Jews being assimilated into German culture. Once defined as such in the popular mind, a major obstacle to Jewish destruction, the common bond in humanity, was overcome.

Social Darwinism took root. This was the tenet that people of different races were in competition with one another, and only the strongest of the races would ultimately survive. [Heinrich Gotthard von] Treitschke, the German philosopher, noted, "The Jews are our misfortune." The expression captured the spirit of the age.[107]

THE SPANISH INQUISITION: SUFFERING INFLICTED

IT WAS IN THE SHADOW of the coming Inquisition that in 1484 Abravanel was summoned to the court of Ferdinand and Isabella. He was there to advise on financial matters, especially on the way to alleviate their vast debts associated with the ongoing war in Granada. His plan, although undefined, won the respect of the monarchs and a place for Abravanel in service to the royals. Only eight years later, the courtier would be faced with expulsion.

When a Jew was baptized and supposedly embraced Christianity, all bigotry was to stop. Unfortunately, that was seldom the case. This was especially true among the burghers (inhabitants of a borough in medieval European cities).[108]

Many burghers were appalled that Jews chose baptism when the real intent had been expulsion from Spain or annihilation. They came to realize much too late that the plan had backfired; the Jews had become candidates for any and all the benefits and status available to other citizens of Spain. Along with that knowledge came the plots and schemes to subject the conversos and Marranos to the same pressures and intimidation heaped upon the non-converted Jews.

Enough years had passed following the riots of 1391 that the conversos had become strongly entrenched in Spanish culture and had often achieved positions of power within the government hierarchy. According to the law, no restrictions could be placed on the new Christians. All the offices of the Church and State were open to them. They became advisers to the king, teachers in the universities, administrative officials, and married into noble families.

The basic so-called "criminal nature" of the converts from Judaism was reason enough for harassment, and the burghers relied on the clergy to find sentient ways based on religious motives to arouse suspicion and create a climate favorable to renewed persecution. The people, unaware that they were being spoon-fed a steady diet of hatred for the converted Jews, yielded to the bureaucratic hype and began to view the conversos and Marranos as religious criminals.

Among these were what came to be known as Crypto-Jews—men and women who "publicly professed Roman Catholicism" but privately adhered to Judaism during the Spanish Inquisition, and particularly after the Alhambra Decree of 1492. Officially they were known as "New Christians," and there was considerable legislation directed against them in both Spain and Portugal and in their colonies, the chief activity of the Inquisition being directed against them.

The pernicious plot to destroy the Marranos was seemingly ignored by the Jewish population, who really had no love for traitors who embraced Catholicism. This was further fueled by the fact that among the Marrano leaders were those who had become staunch enemies of the Jews still residing in Spain. Benzion Netanyahu explained the reaction of the Jews in this way:

> Their medieval religious outlook and reasoning, coupled with their negative attitude toward the Marranos, gave birth to a theory of the Inquisition which was as convenient as it was false. Furthermore, the Marranos, caught in the storm-center of persecution, seemed to have diverted toward themselves most of the enmity for the Jews. . . . Just as

the Jews of Germany failed to foresee Hitler's rise to power at any time during the period preceding that rise, so the Jews of Spain failed to notice, even a few years before the expulsion, the mountainous wave which was approaching to overwhelm them.[109]

The truth is that by the time the edict was handed down, the Marranos had been assimilated into the Catholic culture and had reached the point of no return. It is likely that there were small groups within the larger designation "Marranos" who were secret Jews, but not the majority. Sadly, not only did much of the Church consider the Marranos and conversos as heretics, so did the Jews consider them to be enemies of Judaism. Thus, those caught in the grip of the Inquisition had no champion on either side of the conflict, and no one to stand in their defense. Many historians agree that the majority of the converso community were devoutly Christian and happy with the decision to convert, and that only a small minority were actually crypto-Jews.

In 1478, Pope Sixtus IV sanctioned the Inquisition in Castile to halt what was labeled "the Judaic heresy." The Inquisition was meant to totally uproot all remaining tentacles of Judaism. It would, or so the Church thought, signal the end of any Judaic anomaly that remained in the camp of the conversos and Marranos. On September 27, 1480, Spanish sovereigns Ferdinand and Isabella issued an order to establish tribunals in their kingdom to judge cases of "heretical depravity," the royal decree explicitly stating that the Inquisition was instituted to search out and punish converts to Judaism who transgressed against Christianity by secretly adhering to Jewish beliefs and Jewish rites. According to Benzion Netanyahu:

> The Spanish Inquisition attacked the Marranos with a savage ferocity that by then was outmoded; it burned them by the thousands, confiscated their possessions, incarcerated them in dungeons, branded them as outcasts, robbed their sons of their rightful inheritance while denying them the right to public office, and subjected them all to a reign of terror which "turned their lives into something worse than death," as Mariana, the Spanish historian put it.[110]

So ambitious was Ferdinand that he entertained thoughts of subjugating Italy and France but could not do so without funds. These, he was informed by the Dominicans, could readily be obtained through the Inquisition and the confiscated wealth of Marranos, Moors, and Jews. It would be, he was advised, a blow struck against conversos who were painted as being the enemy of Spain and the Church.

No other faction was cited, no other reason specified. That alone implies an intimate connection between the invention of the Inquisition and the Jews in Spain. To prove the point, Leonardo de Eli, an affluent Jew from Saragossa, was accused and tried, thus exposing Ferdinand's true aims. Sickened by the ploy, Marrano dignitaries introduced petitions to halt the king's plan. The move failed and the Inquisition was strengthened. The desolate Marranos planned and launched a successful scheme to assassinate the Inquisitor in Saragossa. When an outraged Queen Isabella heard of the death, she demanded vengeance on the Marranos. Those seized were hideously persecuted before being slain.

The Church became enmeshed in the racist myth that led its victims inexorably to the dungeon of torture and ultimately the grave. Often the convicted were burned at the stake. As the wood was torched, a choir would sing *Te Deum Laudamus or* "We Praise Thee O Lord." In an atmosphere of greed, fear, and cruelty pursued by Ferdinand and Isabella and sanctioned by the Church, alleged apostates were flushed from their hiding places and dragged through the streets to the place of inquisition. So numerous were the supposed heretics that cellars of monasteries were converted to torture chambers. Frequently the victims were totally unaware of the charges brought against them until they faced the horrors inflicted by the inquisitors.

Once a victim had been charged, tortured, and convicted in a public ceremony, an *auto da fe* (act of faith) was held during which the "heretic" was sentenced and then executed. It was an agonizingly excruciating charade during which the doomed victim was stripped of all humanity before a leering and jeering crowd. Death was doubtless a welcome release from the torture dispensed by the inquisitors.

There was one immense problem that Ferdinand and Isabella failed to consider: As Marranos, conversos, and practicing Jews were arrested and made to suffer torture unto death, the source of funds was dying with them. It was at that point the Church decided to extend mercy to the beleaguered Marranos. During the questionable grace period, all who desired to be reunited with the Church could do so—for a fee. A number of very naïve, or gullible, Marranos accepted the offer only to be forced to reveal the names of other family members who were observant Jews. Again, it was the choice given all too many times to the Jewish people: acquiesce or die.

Pope Sixtus IV, upon hearing reports of the Inquisition, released a papal bull (charter) insisting that modifications be made in the procedures. Ferdinand bristled at the pope's recommendations; the pontiff's interference was a violation of his rights as king and he spurned the order. The pope issued no further writs on the subject.

TOMÁS DE TORQUEMADA, INQUISITOR GENERAL

IT IS NOT REMARKABLE that many wealthy Marranos chose to leave Spain for Portugal and Granada. Ferdinand and Isabella were not especially concerned about outflow, as any treasures abandoned by those fleeing were divvied up by the monarchs and the Church. Disappointed that the gold of the Marranos was insufficient to cover the costs of the Inquisition, church leaders ordered collection boxes placed in the houses of worship where funds were solicited. It had quickly become transparent that a great deal of gold would be needed to arrest, try, and convict innocent men, women, and children.

As the Inquisition gained momentum, one Spaniard managed to carve his name in the annals of history in the blood of Marranos, conversos, and Jews. His name: Tomás de Torquemada of the Spanish Inquisition, of whom more will be written in later chapters. Just as the name Adolf Hitler caused much of the world to cringe when the horrors of the Holocaust were finally revealed, so did the name Torquemada evoke nightmares of a monster in the service of the Church. Writer Anthony Bruno made a comparison among three of history's most notorious murderers: "Qualitatively Torquemada stands shoulder-to-shoulder with Hitler and Stalin."[111]

The bitter irony surrounding his selection to the infamous post of Inquisitor-General is that his grandmother was a Jewish convert to Christianity. Born in Valladolid, Spain, in 1420, Tomás was the nephew of a highly respected theologian, Cardinal Juan de Torquemada, a distinction that would advance his career. A celibate Dominican priest in his early years, Tomás was later appointed Prior at the Monastery Santa Cruz, a station he held until elevated in 1483 to the role of Inquisitor General by Pope Innocent VIII. When Isabella was a child, Tomas developed a close relationship with the future queen as her personal confessor. After she married Ferdinand, Tomás was appointed as a counselor to the royal court.

The Inquisition initially targeted Jews and Moors who

claimed to have converted to Catholicism, a group whose allegiance to the State was questionable. The quest was to ferret out those conversos and Marranos who might possibly be traitors. This distrust ultimately produced the Alhambra Decree underwritten by Torquemada and leading to the Jews being banished from Spain in 1492. During the early years of the Inquisition, Tomás had been limited to targeting only conversos and aggressively urged Ferdinand and Isabella to issue the edict that would force the remaining Spanish Jews to either leave the country or convert.

The deeds of evil men are all too often undergirded by scriptures chosen out of context to substantiate their wicked desires. This was certainly true of the masterminds of the Inquisition who, while searching to authenticate the torture of preference, chose the words of our Lord from John 15:6 (Latin Vulgate and KJV):

> *Si quis in me non manserit mittetur foras*
> *sicut palmes et aruit et colligent eos et in ignem*
> *mittunt et ardent.*

Translation: "If a man abide not in me, he is cast forth as a branch, and is withered; and men gather them, and cast them into the fire, and they are burned."

The horrors were sanctioned by none other than Thomas

Aquinas, who declared: "Heresy is the sin, the guilty of which must be not only excommunicated, but also taken out of the world by death."[112]

Torquemada, in an attempt to clarify the position of Christians toward Jews, cited Psalm 94:14: "For the LORD will not cast off his people, neither will he forsake his inheritance" (KJV).

He declared that the phrases "his people" and "his inheritance" referred solely to Christians, not Jews. Augustine, trying to aid in clarification, determined:

> I do not see how that people [the Jews] could be called the inheritance of God—a people that did not believe in Christ, whom having rejected and slain, they became reprobate; who refused to believe in Him even after His resurrection, and who, in addition, killed His martyrs.[113]

Thomas Aquinas, the noted medieval philosopher and theologian, believed those who failed to support the Inquisition were breaking God's laws. His treatise, "Treatment of Heretics," laid out very stringent measures that were to be taken against anyone accused of heresy.

The Spanish Inquisition thrived on three main

ingredients: bureaucracy, a police force, and a network of informers. This triumvirate from which the participants were drawn each kept a close eye on the other to prevent bribery. The police were held in check by the informers who believed they would secure their own salvation by exposing heretics. It did not hurt that the informers were awarded with no taxation and leniency in the courts. And the informer was also given a portion of the property confiscated from the victim. The informers were presented with a special medal—a cross flanked by a dagger and olive branch—as a sign of their service. They were also allowed to display the emblem on their houses.

Academic Dagobert D. Runes wrote of that terrible time:

> The Spanish Inquisition was perhaps the most cynical plot in the dark history of Catholicism, aimed at expropriating the property of well-to-do Jews and converts in Spain, for the benefit of the royal court and the Church. Even "dead" suspects had their bones dug up for "trial" so estates could be confiscated from their heirs.[114]

As the Inquisition gained momentum in fifteenth-century Spain, the informers were particularly interested in the conversos and ultimately the Marranos. The homes of conversos would be visited on Friday nights in search of signs of Jewish religious activity. Were there lighted candles? Were family members dressed in their best? Either of these was cause for arrest. If no smoke emanated from the chimney on the Jewish Shabbat, it was suspected that the Marranos were practicing Judaism. Suspicions were accompanied by a list of rules by which a backsliding Marrano or converso might be recognized and thus targeted for persecution:

> If they celebrate the Sabbath, wear a clean shirt or better garments, spread a clean table-cloth, light no fire, eat food which has been cooked overnight in the oven, or perform no work on that day; if they eat meat during Lent; if they take neither meat nor drink on the Day of Atonement, go barefoot, or ask forgiveness of another on that day; if they celebrate the Passover with unleavened bread, or eat bitter herbs; if on the Feast of Tabernacles they use green branches or send fruit as gifts to friends; if they marry according to Jewish customs or take Jewish names; if they circumcise their boys . . . if they wash their hands

before praying, bless a cup of wine before
meals and pass it round among the people
at table; if they pronounce blessings while
slaughtering poultry . . . cover the blood with
earth, separate the veins from meat, soak the
flesh in water before cooking, and cleanse it
from blood; if they eat no pork, hare, rabbits,
or eels; if, soon after baptizing a child, they
wash with water the spot touched by the oil;
give Old Testament names to their children
. . . if the women do not attend church within
forty days after confinement; if the dying turn
toward the wall; if they wash a corpse with
warm water; if they recite the Psalms without
adding at the end: "Glory be to the Father, the
Son, and the Holy Ghost."[115]

The inquisitors seemed to entertain a particular hostility toward those conversos who had been appointed by
the Crown to high office. As converts continued to gain
importance in all walks of life, constraints and prejudice rose
against them. By the time the Inquisition was instituted, the
majority of Marranos and conversos had little memory of
the religion that had been practiced by their parents and/or

grandparents. But in the eyes of the Church, they were as guilty as if they had celebrated Passover weeks before. One decree, the *limpieza de sangre* (purity of blood) ordinance stated:

> We declare the so-called conversos, off-spring of perverse Jewish ancestors, must be held by law to be infamous and ignominious, unfit, and unworthy to hold any public office or any benefice within the city of Toledo, or land within its jurisdiction, or to be commissioners for oaths or notaries, or to have any authority over the true Christians of the Holy Catholic Church.[116]

Torquemada was not above using every means available, even falsifying testimony against the Marranos, conversos, and Jews to achieve his objectives. That could not have been more obvious than with the LaGuardia trial, a melodramatic mythological show. The accused were eight conversos and Jews charged with having victimized a Christian child. It had been reported that the condemned had ripped out the heart of a Jewish child in order to summon demon spirits to halt the Inquisition and inflict madness upon Christians. Blatant falsehoods regarding ritual murders of Christians by

Jews have been the source of riots, pograms, and murders for centuries. It is often referred to as "blood libel."

Actually, quite the opposite has been true; professing Christians have often been guilty of ritual murders against Jews—just consider the Spanish Inquisition, where approximately 30,000 Jews were killed. For centuries, the attempts at self-defense by the Marranos went unheard as many of the accused were tried *in absentia* in a charade where only the accusers spoke. Their testimonies languished as the Marranos were summarily convicted and executed. Not until 1873 was the first of those documents published; sadly, it made little difference in public or scholastic opinion.

Not to be confused by facts, Torquemada utilized the LaGuardia trial as a tool to convince Ferdinand and Isabella to implement an order of expulsion against the Jews. Upon receiving word of this plot by the Inquisitor-General, two wealthy Jews raised 30,000 ducats and offered the sum to Ferdinand and Isabella to halt the deportation edict. Always in need of cash, the two sovereigns were tempted to accept the offer when challenged by Torquemada, who cried melodramatically, "Judas sold his Master for thirty ducats. You would sell Him for thirty thousand . . . Take Him and sell Him, but do not let it be said that I have had any share in this transaction."[117]

The accused were tortured until they confessed to a purported crime. They were then burned alive at the stake. Such was the atmosphere in which the Inquisition was launched.

Torquemada firmly believed that conversos and Marranos were progeny of a group of people inclined toward corruption and immorality. They were, therefore, powerless to live a Christian life and should be adjudged to be heretics and were racially inferior.

MISERY, MAYHEM, AND MURDER

MARCOS GARCIA DE MORA was the driving force behind the anti-Marrano movement in Toledo, and as such was its chief spokesman. He urged his followers to adhere to the doctrines of Jesus Christ by robbing the conversos of their possessions and distributing them among the poor—namely the Old Christians. He cavalierly pronounced that some Jewish converts deserved admission into the Christian society, but largely saw a totally different solution to the problem of the Jews in Spain.

Garcia admitted that some of the conversos in Toledo had been victimized because they were traitors and heretics for daring to continue the observance of some Jewish ceremonies. He felt that the punishment meted out was wholly justified and not at all too harsh. He preached that the plot formulated by conversos was to murder the Old Christians, rob them of their possessions, and then surrender the city into the hands of Garcia's enemy, Alvaro de Luna.[118] His charges were not meant to be suppositions but formal charges by which the conversos could be legally tried and executed—by hanging or by being burned at the stake. This, he felt, was a just reward for the traitors who plotted to turn the city over to de Luna and the conversos who supported him.

Garcia justified the methods of killing with "For it is known that they were found to be heretical, infidels and blasphemers of Christ and His Mother . . . those of them who were burned as heretics were justly burned, for the punishment of the heretic—according to divine, human and customary law—is death by fire . . . [and] he who exults in cruelty against criminals for the sake of justice deserves a reward [for] he is a minister of God."[119] He then turned to an expert in canon law to support his interpretation. It was ruled that heretics could be turned over to the secular branch of the Church for the sole purpose of being subjected to due punishment—or burning at the stake. Garcia stated unequivocally that had the Toledans *not* murdered the Marranos, they would have been equally guilty of the crime of omission. He believed their only error was in not annihilating all Marranos and subjecting every converso in the city, and preferably in all of Spain, to a heinous death.

Like many before and after him, Garcia exploited the Scriptures to support his proclamations against the people he saw as heretics and traitors. He saw the role of the Marranos as one of trying to seduce the Old Christians into abandoning their faith. He gave two reasons specifically forbidding the converts from gaining office:

> 1) Because they [conversos] have always played false (*prevaricaron*) in the faith, and *under the guise of Christians* have always done evil and much harm to *true* Christians; and

> 2) Because it is a shady and ugly thing to allow him who yesterday recited prayers in the synagogue to sing today in the church.[120]

The judgments were based on Deuteronomy 24:4–8 and specifically the latter portion of verse 7 (NIV): "You must purge the evil from among you." It gave great latitude to those who were charged with defining "evil."

The word *inquisition* came to be known and feared throughout medieval Europe, but perhaps it was the Spanish

Inquisition that was synonymous with ruthlessness, fierceness, and depravity. From the issuance of the papal bull by Pope Sixtus IV, Ferdinand and Isabella began to wield the scythe of destruction against Marranos, conversos, and Jews in Spain with the express purpose of rooting out counterfeit Christians. The two sovereigns sparred for a time over the tribunals that were to be established to conduct the Inquisition. The pope and Isabella ultimately won the day, and Ferdinand acquiesced to the wishes of his wife and the head of the Church. (It appears that Isabella may have, at times, rivaled Queen Jezebel.[121]) An explicit target was those Jews and Moors who had claimed conversion to Christianity but who were, it was charged, still clandestine practitioners of their faith. Nor were the sovereigns shy about collecting any income generated by the Inquisition—from confiscated lands, jewels, gold, and other sources.

It is often thought—quite erroneously—that the Inquisition lasted only a few years; the truth is that it lasted until 1834, an inconceivable 384 years. At that time, then Queen Mother Cristina declared, ". . . the Tribunal of the Inquisition is definitely suppressed."[122]

The methods used by the inquisitors during the Spanish

Inquisition were understandably horrifying. Citizens were coerced into delivering friends, neighbors, business associates, and even family members into the hands of the torturers because of some real or perceived crime against the Church. Those who faced the inquisitors had little recourse: They could not engage a lawyer to plead their case; the name of their accuser could not be revealed; even the charges against the accused could not be known. Confessions were extracted by the most heinous of tortures.

In *The History of the Christian Church*, author William Jones quoted Voltaire:

> Their form of proceeding is an infallible way to destroy whomsoever the inquisitors wish. The prisoners are not confronted with the accuser or informer; nor is there any informer or witness who is not listened to. A public convict, a notorious malefactor, an infamous person, a common prostitute, a child, are in the holy office, though nowhere else, credible accusers and witnesses. Even the son may depose against his father, the wife against her husband.[123]

Following the cessation of the Inquisition, no other such

brutal and aggressive methods were employed by any power in Western civilization for scarcely one hundred years until the rise of the Third Reich in Germany and the Communists in Soviet countries.

Those charged with carrying out the Inquisition appeared to hold a singular animosity toward conversos and Marranos who held stations of authority in the courts and financial institutions. Often a Jew was appointed to the position of the King's Chief Treasurer, a place of great trust. The man in that chair was often gifted with monetary proficiencies and an extensive knowledge of the numerous challenges that influenced economic situations. These assignments were a basis for acrimonious hostility that some Christian aristocrats felt toward Jews who held positions of power within the court.

Men, women, and even children from every stratum were caught in the inquisitors' trap, having been sent there because of the jealousy or hatred of another. The thoroughness and brutality of the Inquisition seemed to particularly target and entrap the greatest number of Jews.

How the words *inquisition* and *church* could conceivably be used in the same sentence has puzzled historians for centuries. How could a religion that teaches love, tolerance, grace, and mercy be even remotely connected to the monstrous torture of having individuals burned alive or tortured in the most foul and horrifying ways? How could fanatical minions of the Church misinterpret Scripture in order to justify their actions? In a questionable attempt to find a biblical basis for its acts, leaders turned to Titus 3:10–11 (KJV):

> A man that is an heretick after the first and second admonition reject; Knowing that he that is such is subverted, and sinneth, being condemned of himself.

The routine for the Inquisitor-General seldom varied. Torquemada, overseer of fifteen district tribunals in Spain, and his train of fifty mounted bodyguards accompanied by 200 foot soldiers would ride majestically into a town or village. But so paranoid was the cleric that he often kept a charm nearby, a unicorn's horn, said to protect him from poisoning.[124] Torquemada would unleash his silver-tongued rhetoric in the town square or local church. His topic: the evils of heresy. The list of tenets regarding how to spot a sinner would be distributed, including instructions as to what to do should a heretic be discovered. It was, frankly, the perfect opportunity to cause havoc in the lives of enemies— real or perceived.

A grace period of several weeks would follow the debacle in the square during which involuntary confessions among the populace were urged. During this time, testimony of an individual's heresy was solicited from witnesses that numbered as few as one or as many as thousands. The person who came forward and admitted heretical behavior was given less-severe punishment. Those who chose to rely on the mercy of the court were severely disappointed.

After accusations were received by the inquisitors, the individual was bidden to appear before the Inquisition. It was not a mandatory appearance, but failure to do so was perceived as guilt. According to historians Miroslav Hroch and Ann Skybova, there was ample advice on how to handle the interrogation of an accused:

> The Inquisitor should behave in a friendly manner and act as though he already knows the whole story. He should glance at his papers and say, "It's quite clear you are not telling the truth." Or should pick up a document and look surprised, saying: "How can you lie to me like this when what I've got written down here contradicts everything you've told me?" He should then continue:

"Just confess—you can see that I know the whole story already."[125]

Secrecy was the order of the day. No information was released to the suspect, although it was not uncommon for a list of those who might carry grudges against them to be solicited. If the names of the accusers appeared on the list, the accused *might* be released. It behooved the suspect to present lengthy lists to the Inquisitor-General. It was not permitted to call witnesses in rebuttal to the charges, and if a lawyer was permitted, he could be charged as an accessory if the person was convicted of the crime.

The accused were placed in solitary confinement, often for three or four years, with contact limited only to the inquisitors. All expenses associated with the incarceration had to be paid by the defendant. That, coupled with the fact that those adjudged guilty were stripped of their property, was a prime reason the wealthy were often targeted by the Inquisition. The indicted were harassed to confess to heresy in order to save their souls, and if guilt was admitted, they were pressed to reveal the names of other potential heretics. They were then often released with only penances to be paid. In Spain the penance could include scourging or lashing and being forced to wear a large yellow cross, or *sanbenito*.

The severest judgments—burning at the stake or total loss of property—were earmarked for those who refused to renounce their heresy or, as in Spain, conversos who continued to secretly practice their faith. Once convicted, the "relapsed" heretic was handed off to secular authorities for punishment in order to spare the Church from having to administer the death penalty. This was based on an ancient principle of the Church: *ecclesia abhorret a sanguine* ("the Church shrinks from blood").[126] Thus, the preferred method of execution—burning at the stake; no blood was shed. (In Spain, offspring of heretics could not hold public office, join holy orders, become doctors, teachers of the young, or lawyers.)

Torture was employed beginning in 1252 after having been authorized by Pope Innocent IV, and approximately one-third of all individuals charged with heresy in Spain were subjected to torture.[127] After an admission of heresy was extracted by the most painful means, the accused would be forced to verify his/her confession. Refusal meant back to the torture chamber.

The inquisitors invented or customized techniques of torture designed to extract confessions—whether valid or not. The methods were designed to inflict the most pain possible just short of death. These horrific torture devices included:

✧ The Strappado: The victim's hands were tied behind his back and a rope attached by which he was suspended and repeatedly raised and dropped.

✧ The Rack: a rectangular frame with rollers at both ends. The victim's hands and feet were secured to the rollers by ropes. A handle attached to the rollers was used to ratchet the ropes/chains tighter and tighter, slowly and excruciatingly dislocating the joints.

✧ The Judas Chair: a pyramid-shaped seat, the point of which was inserted into the anus. The defendant was slowly lowered farther and farther onto the seat by overhead ropes.

✧ The Boot: a wooden shoe placed on the victim's foot and tightened incrementally, crushing the bones of the foot and lower leg.

✧ The Thumbscrew: similar to the boot but used to crush hands and fingers.

✧ The Breast Ripper: a large claw capable of ripping a woman's breast from her body.[128]

✧ Waterboarding: The accused was bound to a board placed in a slightly downward angle—the feet higher than the head. The victim's hands and feet were tightly secured so that the bindings cut into the flesh if there was any movement at all. The head was held firmly in place by a band of metal and the mouth forced open with a length of iron. Wood was inserted into the nostrils, and a length of cloth placed over the mouth. Water was slowly poured into the accused's mouth so that each time he was forced to swallow, part of the cloth was ingested. Just prior to drowning or suffocation, the inquisitor would yank the cloth from the mouth and begin the process again. After a lengthy torture session, bits of the cloth would adhere to the intestines and the victim would be eviscerated. (This method of torture has a frightening similarity to modern-day methods. Perhaps humanity has not advanced as much as has been thought.)

The writhing, half-dead victims were sarcastically addressed as "Brother in Christ" while every means possible was used—without mercy or any pretense of concern—to extract a confession. These devices of torment were given inoffensive labels to mask the very character of the monstrous actions with which they were associated. The place in which the persecution was inflicted was called *Casa Santa*, or "holy house."

In a nearby cathedral, a priest celebrated Mass as the prisoner was dragged from his place of confinement. Bells were rung as the procession slowly marched toward the place of execution, the doomed arrayed in white robes and the anguish endured described as a rite of "purification." In some villages, flames of fire and horrible devil-like creatures were painted on the garments. Each victim was made to parade to the funeral pyre in the town square carrying a tall candle.

The parade-like atmosphere was enhanced by nobles on horseback and members of the Inquisitor-General's contingent accompanying the condemned. The judged were forced to bow their knees and place their hands on a prayer book as they repeated their coerced confession. The victim was then excommunicated from the Church before the sentence was carried out.

As Inquisitor-General during the reign of Ferdinand and Isabella, Tomás Torquemada was described by Spanish chronicler Sebastián de Olmedo perhaps derisively as "the hammer of heretics, the light of Spain, the savior of his country, the honor of his order."[129] Author Jane Gerber wrote:

> Ironically, the horror of this first decade of the Inquisition caused a recoil in the *converso* population that sent many of them back to their Jewish roots. The religion and tradition that was painted as a crime by the Christians in Spain became again a source of honor and pride to the Sephardim. In fact, Jews became increasingly willing to risk even the pyre of the *auto-da-fe* in order to remain faithful to the God of Israel.[130]

The Inquisition was not confined to Spain. Its effects were felt in France, England, Portugal, Brazil, and in the American colonies.[131]

THOSE WHO GO DOWN
TO THE SEA IN SHIPS...[132]

CHRISTOPHER COLUMBUS, explorer extraordinaire, arrived in Spain in 1484 only to face the horror and infamy of the Inquisition. He had been introduced to the court of Ferdinand and Isabella and had prepared a presentation to the sovereigns. His hope was to receive their blessing—and financing—to follow the setting sun west in search of a route to Asia.

Not surprisingly, the Inquisition had provoked a fever of exploration. Who wouldn't want an opportunity to escape the insanity that had gripped Spain? What better time for Columbus to make his bid for a voyage of exploration. Even as the discussions between King Ferdinand and Queen Isabella were being held, the momentous decree of expulsion evicting all Jews from Spain was being composed for the monarchs. When confronted with the cruel truth of ejection, two of the nation's foremost statesmen and civic leaders, Abraham Seneor and Don Isaac Abravanel, fought to have the writ overturned. Seneor, the court rabbi and chief tax collector of Spain, had functioned as a significant go-between during the engagement of the two sovereigns and provided funds for the gift that sealed the matrimonial match between the pair. Abravanel, his associate and beneficiary, had earned the respect of the highest politicos due to his financial advice. He was also thought to have been one of the leading Jewish scholars of his day. The king, willing to attend to the two, accepted a significant bribe from Abravanel—which had no effect on the outcome. Abravanel wrote of his plea to the monarchs to halt the expulsion order:

> I pleaded with the king many times. I sup-
> plicated him thus: "Save O king, Why do this
> to thy servants? Lay on us every tribute and
> ransom, gold and silver and everything that
> the children of Israel possess they shall will-
> ingly give to their fatherland." I sought out
> my friends, those who stood near the king

and enjoy his confidence, and begged them to beseech and petition him to revoke the evil decree concerning our destruction and annihilation, but all in vain. Like an adder which stoppeth its ears, he remained deaf to our appeals. The queen, also, was standing by his side, but she would not listen to our plea. On the contrary, she argued in favor of carrying out the plan. I neither rested nor speared [sic] myself, yet the calamity was not averted.[133]

Thinking only of his rapidly declining coffers and ways to refill them, Ferdinand obviously gave little consideration to the future of his kingdom. He cared not at all for the fact that Spain was being stripped of one of its most precious natural resources—the Sephardic Jews. In his bid to appease the Church and empower the State, Ferdinand was quick to relinquish the treasure of scientists, craftsmen, physicians, solicitors, educators, poets, and inventors.

While the king was surrendering to the idol of greed, Columbus rapidly validated himself among the most conspicuous converso figures in the court of the Spanish rulers. (As with Abravanel, Seneor, Santangel, and Gabriel

Sanchez, other Jewish converts to Christianity who served the empire included Alfonso de la Caballeria, vice chancellor and political associate of Aragon, and Juan Cabrero, royal administrator.) Apparently, these noblemen were still thought to be trustworthy and were engaged as loyal retainers of Ferdinand and Isabella, even though the Inquisition was an ever-present and threatening demon lurking in the background, waiting to rear its ugly head in condemnation of the conversos.

Attempts to execute conversos and Marranos during the Inquisition were, it seemed, not enough to satisfy the royals. Following the fall of Granada, reports began to spread in court factions that an expulsion decree to banish all unconverted Jews would soon be enacted. Precise dates for the endeavor have been debated, but it was likely signed near the end of January 1492. It was following the definite proclamation of the order that Santangel and Abravanel tried unsuccessfully to compel Ferdinand to withdraw the decree. The king refused to alter his decision and Isabella prodded him to maintain his determination to deport all Jews from Spain.

As the fiery Jewish leader stood before the court in defense of his people, Abravanel was described by Capsali and other historians:

There he stood like a lion in wisdom and strength, and in the most eloquent language he addressed the king and queen. . . . [He] decided to write [his] words down and to send them to Queen Isabella . . . Thus Don Abravanel sent a letter to Queen Isabella, in which he chastised her mercilessly and showed no respect for her rank. He then arranged to have the letter delivered to the queen while he fled for his life.[134]

In an attempt to stay the departure of Don Isaac Abravanel and Seneor, Ferdinand and Isabella devised a plan to have Abravanel's grandson kidnapped, hoping that the family would convert to Catholicism and remain in Spain. Don Isaac was warned of the conspiracy and had the child sent to a relative in Portugal. Abravanel refused to be blackmailed. Seneor was not as strong-willed as his friend; he converted, adopted the name Coronel, and was baptized, an event gladly attended by the monarchs.[135]

Author Yitzhak Baer, however, provides more insight into what many saw as Seneor's capitulation to pressure from the Crown:

The queen had sworn if Don Abraham

Seneor were not baptized, she would destroy all the Jewish communities; he did what he did to save the lives of many people, not of his own desire. His son-in-law also followed his example, for both of them fell victim to the queen's design, they having reared her and made her great.[136]

Some scholars believe the expulsion decree was an effort to rid Spain of those thought to be infidels as defined by the Catholic Church. Others point out that the decree appears to be a wholesale invitation to conversion, allowing those who chose to convert to keep their status and riches. There are those who believe Ferdinand was indeed a cunning and greedy monarch who was quite shrewd at hiding his brutality behind a mask of religious sanctimoniousness. He actually protected his Jewish subjects during the 1470s and 1480s while apparently plotting their expulsion. Ferdinand borrowed large sums from Abravanel and his brethren to pay for the war to retake Granada, then scurrilously ousted them before the debt came due. It is said that Abravanel enjoyed such wealth that he was able to loan the monarchs a tenth of the 12,000,000 reals offered them. He apparently felt blessed that his fortune exceeded that of his ancestors, but after the expulsion his enormous assets—land, jewels, gold, and more—were confiscated by Ferdinand.

Of course, some historians believe Ferdinand and Isabella were coerced into making the move to exorcise the Jews by Tomás de Torquemada, while others think Isabella was the determining factor and compare her to the wicked and idolatrous biblical Queen Jezebel.

Capsali wrote of her betrayal of the Jewish people:

> Actually, Isabella had always hated the Jews, and had been involved in an ongoing argument with her husband Ferdinand, for ever since her marriage she had been asking him to exile the Jews of Spain. In this the king was spurred on by the priests . . . When, however, she saw that the king was reluctant to take such a step, she told him: "You no doubt love the Jews, and the reason is that you are of their flesh and blood. In fact, the reason the Jews arranged for you to marry me is so that you would act as their protector." When the King heard this terrible thing, he took his shoe off and threw it at the Queen, hitting her. She then fled the room and the

hatred between them continued for a long period of time.[137]

Imagine, if you can, how the Jews and conversos must have felt when the decree ordering them out of Spain was published abroad. They were given four months to wrap up their affairs while being forbidden to take their gold, silver, and jewels with them as they fled. The Jews were forced to try to rid themselves of property—homes, lands, vineyards, grain fields, and shops. They had built stunning houses of worship, ceremonial bathhouses, and public rooms. It was impossible for them to pedal their possessions in a glutted market where a villa sold for the price of a donkey and diamonds for the price of a linen handkerchief. It is said that some buried their possessions hoping they would be able to return at a later date to repossess their property.

Don Isaac Abravanel and his son-in-law were among the few who were actually granted permission to take the sum of two thousand ducats each in gold and jewelry, a paltry amount for their vast holdings but nearly the equivalent of two million dollars in today's market. In so doing, Abravanel relinquished the right to collect any outstanding debts owed him upon his departure from Spain.

He wrote of the despair that gripped the Jewish community:

> The people heard this evil decree and they mourned. Wherever word of the decree reached, there was great mourning among the Jews. There was great trembling and sorrow the likes of which had not been experienced since the days of the exile of the Jews from their land to the land of foreigners. The Jews encouraged each other: Let us strengthen ourselves on behalf of our faith, on behalf of the Torah of our God . . . if [our enemies] let us live, we will live; and if they kill us, we will die. But we will not profane our covenant, and our hearts will not retrogress; we will walk forward in the name of the Lord our God.[138]

The real challenge was in finding another country in Europe or elsewhere that would welcome these Jewish outcasts from Spain. They were rejected by England, France, Germany, and Italy. North Africa was a possibility for asylum, but getting there was a challenge at which many failed, as they were victimized by treacherous sea captains in ships that were less than seaworthy. Author Simon Wiesenthal wrote of an anecdote that dated from 1938 and Hitler's invasion of Austria. He told of a Jewish man who enters a travel agency in Vienna seeking a country to which he might emigrate. The agent sets a globe on the counter and draws an imaginary line from country to country as she recounts the reasons the Jew might not be welcome there. As she exhausts the possibilities, the Jewish man asks, "Is that the only globe you have?"[139]

All Jews regardless of age were ordered to depart by July 31—the day before *Tisha B'Av*—the yearly day of fasting for the Jews. It is an observance of the destruction of the first and second temples in Jerusalem, and is said to be the saddest day of the Hebrew calendar. Luis De Torres, a Marrano, wrote in his diary:

> Three hundred thousand people, half the amount that were redeemed from Egyptian slavery, descended to the Mediterranean shore, searching for passage to a new land, to a land where they could openly practice Judaism. I was among them.
>
> However, I was not a refugee; I had been commissioned to join Christopher Columbus's voyage of discovery. I agreed to accompany

him because I hoped that if we found Jewish brethren, I would be able to live my life in peace and in freedom. Don Rodriguez, his uncle Don Gabriel Sanchez, Alonso de Loquir, Rodrigo de Triana, Chon Kabrera, Doctor Briena and Doctor Marco, all agreed with my reasoning and joined, but except for Rodrigo, they sailed on the other ships. We were a large group of conversos (Marranos), living in perpetual fear of the Inquisition, hoping that we would find a way out of the precarious situation we were in . . .

Columbus thought that when he would reach China and the Far East, he would locate the exiled Jews from the Ten Lost Tribes, and he wanted me [with a knowledge of Hebrew] to be able to communicate with them.[140]

Prior to the expulsion date, an exchange of letters was said to have taken place between Jewish leaders in Spain and those in Constantinople. The subject: What should the Jews do to protect themselves under such intolerable conditions? The Jewish head in Constantinople allegedly replied that they were to implement various methods including training their sons as financiers in order to strip the Old Christians of their wealth; learning the art of medicine in order to execute their patients; feign conversion until such time as they could continue to practice Judaism. Copies of the supposed documents were presented to the pope as evidence against the Jews to confirm the malevolence of conversos. There is no evidence to support the erroneous conclusion reached by the Church that Jews in Spain followed the council of their brethren in Constantinople.

The first week in July was the beginning of the end for many of the Jewish families in Spain. They were permitted to take their property provided it was not in gold, silver, or money, which left little other than clothing or livestock. Though some were welcomed in Portugal, King John II only allowed them sanctuary for eight months, after which they had to be prepared to move yet again—or face mandatory conversion, as they had in Spain.

The stories accompanying those who were targeted by Ferdinand and Isabella as well as King John II are heart-rending. According to author Jane Gerber, some set out on their journey for the coast but turned back to accept conversion in the panic that followed; some were threatened by Isabella with harsh consequences if they refused to convert, among them Abraham Seneor, the leading Jewish courtier; others were forcibly converted in Portugal upon threat of being enslaved. Samuel Usque, a Portuguese Jewish historian, wrote of the horrors that faced Jewish parents as their children were literally wrested from their arms and auctioned to the highest bidders on the island of São Tomé near West Africa:

> [The island] was inhabited by lizards, snakes, and other venomous reptiles and was devoid of rational beings. Here the king exiled condemned criminals, and he decided to include among them the innocent children of these Jews. . . .
>
> When the luckless hour arrived for this barbarity to be inflicted, mothers scratched their faces in grief as their babes, less than three years old, were taken from their arms . . . The fated children raised their piercing cries to heaven as they were mercilessly torn from their beloved parents . . . One mother, distraught by this horrible unexplained cruelty, lifted her baby in her arms, and paying no heed to its cries, threw herself from the

ship into the heaving sea, and drowned embracing her only child. . . .

Finally, when those innocent children arrived at the wilderness of São Tomé, which was to be their grave, they were thrown ashore and were mercilessly left there. Almost all were swallowed up by the huge lizards on the island and the remainder, who escaped these reptiles, wasted away from hunger and abandonment.[141]

Centuries before the expulsion in Spain, the prophet Jeremiah also mourned the loss of Israel's children:

A voice was heard in Ramah, lamentation and bitter weeping, Rachel weeping for her children, refusing to be comforted for her children, because they are no more. (Jeremiah 31:15 NKJV)

As the Jews prepared for the march to the Mediterranean it was Don Isaac Abravanel, joined by rabbis and other counselors, who helped arrange conveyances for their dispossessed countrymen. They arranged for the ships that would take them to Africa, Turkey, and Italy. The people marched forward, the conversos believing that their expulsion was the prelude to the coming of the Messiah. It has been said that the roads along the way were lined with priests begging the Jews to convert. That tactic was thwarted by the treatment—the Inquisition, the torture, the suspicion, the distrust—many had received at the hands of the so-called "Old Christians" of the Church. Why should they believe that anything would be different if they were to submit to a last-minute conversion?

Benzion Netanyahu wrote of the aftermath of the expulsion in his book about Abravanel. He said of King Ferdinand:

> Having come to the conclusion . . . that Spain could not absorb Jews or Marranos, he wanted to be the one to effect their liquidation, and with maximum immediate advantage . . . The immediate profits of the expulsion of the Jews were incomparably greater than any possible increase in the revenues which the Jews might have brought in decades. . . . Some 7,000,000 maravedis were collected after the expulsion by the government from the moneys and sale of houses and valuables left behind by the Jews in Burgos

alone!... The expulsion of the Jews presented to them [Ferdinand and Isabella] a way of settling their financial difficulties.[142]

A vast number of Jews gathered at the docks awaiting a berth, no matter how cramped, on ships that could be expected to do little more than remain afloat. The only slightly seaworthy crafts were jammed with the bodies of terrified, saddened, and hopeless individuals. After days at sea confined in such close quarters, disease was rampant. The threat of an epidemic kept many of the ill-fated refugees stranded on beaches where scores either died from illness or starved. So desperate were some that they opted to return to Spain and accept forced conversion if it meant being able to feed their children. In his volume on the life of Don Isaac Abravanel, Benzion Netanyahu quoted Genoese historian Bartolomeo Senarega on the condition of the émigrés:

> One might have taken them for specters, so emaciated were they, so cadaverous in their aspect, and with eyes so shrunken; they differed in nothing from the dead except in the power of motion, which indeed they scarcely retained.[143]

Surely in looks they resembled those freed from Nazi concentration camps at the end of World War II; and perhaps they felt much as the children of Israel had after leaving Egypt and trekking into the wilderness of Sinai. They lamented to Moses, "Why did you bring us out here to die in the wilderness? Weren't there enough graves for us in Egypt?" (Exodus 14:11 NLT). The people might have cried, "Weren't there enough graves for us in Spain?"

Italy was one of the few countries that made provision for the exiles. Ferrante (Ferdinand I), the king of Naples, allowed the weary travelers to land. Hospitals were set up to treat the pestilence that had gripped the Jews as they journeyed and food was provided for the hungry. It was on the Italian shore that Abravanel set foot. It is a testament to his greatness that he did not long languish in obscurity. He was soon offered a place in the king's court, and later referred to the monarch and his son as "princes of mercy and righteousness."[144] He served in the court until near the end of his life when he was driven to Turkey after the deposing of Ferrante's son and heir to the throne, Alfonso.

Far too many of the exiles were forced to cross the Mediterranean to the shores of northern Africa, where they were relegated to insect-infested straw huts that sat outside the safety of the walls of towns and villages. Again, many died of starvation, their orphaned children forced into slavery. Other ports of call accepted the Jews on the basis that they convert to Christianity, and their own brethren rejected them for fear of contracting diseases—including the Plague. There were some, however, who sold their possessions in order to feed their colleagues and, in some instances, liberate them from bondage. When the final ship had landed and the last Jew disembarked, they and their ancestors could be found in Europe and in the New World continents of North and South America, in North Africa, and in the Indies.

ROME AND REFORMATION

THE SIXTEENTH CENTURY debuted with only one religious group holding authority in Western Europe—the Roman Catholic Church. It was both opulent and omnipotent. The pope and priests held formidable power over the adherents. It was not long, however, before discontent began to seep into the Church in matters such as interpretive policies. For example, were only priests and teachers endowed with the right to illuminate the Scriptures for the people? It had become the belief of some during the fourteenth century that the common man had the right to read and interpret the Bible for himself.

Men such as John Wycliffe, a priest/educator at Oxford, and Czech priest/philosopher John Hus delivered powerful sermons outlining their ideology that the Bible should be available to all. The philosophies of these two men, in particular, greatly influenced Martin Luther, a Saxon monk who would have a profound effect on the Catholic Church.

As the inevitable clashed headlong with the immovable, Jews in Europe were few. There were none in England following the 1290 expulsion or in Spain after the edict signed by Ferdinand and Isabella in 1492. The wholesale murder of Jews in Germany was tied to the Lenten observance in 1349, and decimated the number in that country. Professor Eric W. Gritsch of Lutheran Theological Seminary wrote:

> The slanderous medieval propaganda against Jews was revived by a bestselling book published in 1530, *The Whole Jewish Faith (Der ganze jüdische Glaub)*. Its author was Anthony Margaritha, a Jew who had converted to Lutheranism in 1522. . . . Margaritha became a source for Luther's own radical polemics against the Jews. . . . But strong supporters of Luther's Reformation did not share his radical anti-Semitism . . .[145]

Luther made his presence known to the Catholic Church when, in 1517, he posted his Ninety-five Theses on the door of a church in Wittenberg, Germany. He railed against "indulgences" or the sale of pardons for various sins, leaving repentance completely out of the equation. Rejecting papal authority, Luther, like his champions Wycliffe and Hus, declared the Bible to be the sole authority of truth. He petitioned for the abolition of monasteries and convents, and declared that vows taken by nuns and priests —including those of celibacy—were nonbinding. Luther reduced the seven sacraments observed by the Church to two: baptism and the Eucharist (Lord's Supper).

Luther's challenge to the Church was simply a reflection of the unrest that was sweeping through Europe—a rebellion against Charles V, head of the Holy Roman Empire. Laborers and merchants alike believed the Church favored the tyrants who ruled over them. Unrest seethed under the surface, threatening to erupt into chaos. Luther's defiance became the coalescing point behind which people could unite. By 1530, the momentum had abated and some of Luther's support had evaporated, but the Reformation had become a fixture that even he could no longer control. From the protests that surrounded the Reformation, the word *Protestant* came into popular usage.

In 1523, Luther penned a treatise titled, "That Jesus Christ Was Born A Jew." In an excerpt, Luther suggested, at that time:

Therefore, I would request and advise that one deal gently with them and instruct them from Scripture; then some of them may come along. Instead of this we are trying only to drive them by force, slandering them, accusing them of having Christian blood if they don't stink, and I know not what other foolishness. So long as we thus treat them like dogs, how can we expect to work any good among them? Again, when we forbid them to labor and do business and have any human fellowship with us, thereby forcing them into usury, how is that supposed to do them any good?[146]

Luther decried the idea of the "blood libel" attributed to Jewish customs; he criticized the tactics of passionate priests who used Easter celebrations to castigate the Jews as "Christ killers." He exhibited a notable sympathy toward his Jewish countrymen. It was his wish that Jews would realize that Jesus was the Messiah and convert willingly, not by coercion or affliction. Rejection of his overtures took Martin Luther down a totally different path, one paved with anti-Semitism and vitriol.

Twenty years later, however, Luther's outlook had changed dramatically. There were purported to be several reasons for his drastic about-face regarding Jews:

✧ The rejection of his kind overtures and his wish to see them converted.

✧ The peasant uprisings in 1524–1525 provoked by "a combination of several factors, including changes in social and economic structures, heavy taxation by both the nobility and [the] Catholic Church, religious changes engendered by the Reformation, and a crisis of the old feudal system."[147] The peasants targeted three entities: their overlords, priests, and of course, Jews.

✧ The charges against Luther of having become a "Judaizer," because of his interpretation of the Old Testament—one that was diametrically opposite of the Roman clergy.[148]

So distressed was Luther at the lack of response by Jews, and by the charges leveled against him from other quarters that he became totally disenchanted with the Jewish people, and turned against them. In a homily titled, "On the Jews and Their Lies," the reformer emasculated them with his pen. Four hundred years before Adolf Hitler introduced the Nuremburg Laws (September 1935), Luther set the following to parchment:

> What shall we Christians do with this rejected and condemned people, the Jews? Since they live among us, we dare not tolerate their conduct, now that we are aware of their lying and reviling and blaspheming. If we do, we become sharers in their lies, cursing and blasphemy. . . . I shall give you my sincere advice:
>
> First to set fire to their synagogues or schools and to bury and cover with dirt whatever will not burn, so that no man will ever again see a stone or cinder of them. . . .
>
> Second, I advise that their houses also be razed and destroyed. . . .
>
> Third, I advise that all their prayer books and Talmudic writings, in which such idolatry, lies, cursing and blasphemy are taught, be taken from them. . . .
>
> Fourth, I advise that their rabbis be

forbidden to teach henceforth on pain of loss
of life and limb. . . .

Fifth, I advise that [safe-conduct] on the
highways be abolished completely for the
Jews. . . .

Sixth, I advise that usury be prohibited to
them, and that all cash and treasure of silver
and gold be taken from them and put aside
for safekeeping. . . .

Seventh, I commend putting a flail, an ax,
a hoe, a spade, a distaff, or a spindle into the
hands of young, strong Jews and Jewesses
and letting them earn their bread in the sweat
of their brow, as was imposed on the children
of Adam. . . .[149]

In her Masters Thesis, Rollins College scholar Daphne
Olsen compared Luther and Hitler:

The shared similarities between Luther
and Hitler were not limited to their hatred
for anything Jewish, however. Both men were
led by a strong sense of German nationalism
and a yearning for unity among their fellow
Germans.

Why was such romantic nationalism anti-Semitic in particular? Why single out the Jews? The answer is quite clear: everybody 'knew' that the Jews were the enemy of German civilization, because the Germans, like other Europeans, had been taught over the long Christian centuries that the Jews were the enemy of Christian civilization. [Olsen cited William Nicholls, *Christian Antisemitism: A History of Hate*, 346.][150]

Luther's fits of vitriolic linguistics have been duly noted by several apologists. Author Peter Wiener wrote:

Luther's language was indeed something quite abominable and indescribable. "He is obsessed with filth and obscenity," writes Maritain. To call it "revolutionary journalism" is an understatement. "He would be furiously angry, and when he was angry he fairly vomited filth. He wrote things one cannot quote in decent English," is much nearer to the mark. This again, was only the natural outcome of his neurotic character. There was nothing godlike or holy about him, there was little patience or human understanding; he loved to scream, shout and blaspheme in the manner of the most vulgar German politician, such as our generation has seen more than enough. With pride he himself exclaimed; "Rage acts as a stimulant to my whole being. It sharpens my wits, puts a stop to the assaults of the Devil and drives out care. Never do I write or speak better than when I am in a rage. If I wish to compose, write, pray and preach well, I have to be in a rage" ("Table Talk," 1210).[151]

Luther became a proponent of what we today call "replacement theology," or "supersessionism," a doctrine that has filtered down through the centuries to the modern church. Replacement theology feeds anti-Semitism through ignorance and lack of understanding. For instance, the Jews were labeled "Christ killers" because of the crucifixion. This led to attacks of every imaginable nature being launched against them. They have constantly faced lack, banishment, attacks, or the threat of eradication.

I believe any theological idea that separates Christians from their Jewish roots is unscriptural, with the practical result being that it stunts their spiritual understanding and growth. Supersessionism is defined as ...

> The theological concept that, because the vast majority of Jews in the first century CE did not accept Jesus as their Messiah, God unilaterally terminated His covenants with the Jewish people and transferred them to the followers of Christianity. It relegates Judaism to an inferior position and recognizes Christianity as the "true" or "spiritual" Israel.[152]

Replacement theology rejects the concept that the promises God made to Israel are for this present hour; that instead, they were canceled at Calvary. As a result, this doctrine contends, these promises now fall to the church, which has replaced Israel. The absurdity of this dogma is that if Christian leaders believe God ended His promises to the Jewish people, they must also believe He might revoke His promises to them as well!

What exactly do supersessionists believe?

- ✧ They tend to be anti-Israel, and therefore do not honor Israel.

- ✧ They tend to be pro-Palestinian.

✧ They marginalize Christians who support Israel, even with humanitarian
issues.

Obviously, these theologians have abandoned the apostle
Paul's teaching to the Romans. He wrote in Romans 11:1–2
(NKJV):

> I say then, has God cast away His people?
> Certainly not! For I also am an Israelite, of
> the seed of Abraham, of the tribe of Benja-
> min. God has not cast away His people whom
> He foreknew. Or do you not know what the
> Scripture says of Elijah, how he pleads with
> God against Israel?

In actuality, Martin Luther was not the first to embrace
the doctrine of replacement theology. It was first developed
by Justin Martyr (circa AD 100–165) and Irenaeus of Lyon
(circa AD 130–200). Origen espoused the theory of allegoriza-
tion—or the use of a parable to explain an event. For instance,
he taught that in the triumphal entry the foal was used to
symbolize the New Testament gospel. The two apostles sent
to fetch the colt were representative of humanity.

Doesn't it follow, then, that if the donkey was indicative
of the Old Testament and the foal, the New Testament, the

Israel of the Old Testament is now the church of the New? Such machinations disavow the literal interpretation of the Bible and allows the preacher, teacher, or priest to cause the Scriptures to say whatever they wish.

This was largely accepted within the church by the fourth century, and has led to a great deal of persecution of Jews by Christians. Some Protestant reformers, however, began to question this practice by the end of the 1500s. Replacement theology, like other misconceptions, rears its head from time to time in an attempt to disavow the relevance of Israel. Although the Catholic Church reversed its stance on replacement theology in the twentieth century, many conservative Protestant groups still ascribe to this doctrine.

As in earlier centuries, at times the church has been a willing participant in the genocide perpetrated against the Jews. From the times of the early Catholic Church to the Crusades, from Martin Luther's Reformation to World War II, the church has sometimes been duplicitous in the terrorizing of Jews.

Embracing replacement theology has led to rampant anti-Semitism in some Christian churches. Jews have continuously faced lack, banishment, violence, or the threat of eradication.

This devious doctrine propagates the age-old practice of blaming the Jews for the world's ills, weighing them in the balance and finding them wanting. It also frees these misled believers from their responsibility to share the good news of the gospel of Jesus Christ with all whom He came to seek and to save.

In that the concept of replacement theology is still taught in modern times, I wrote in *The American Prophecies*:

> By replacing literal Israel in the Bible with the Church, Christians of the time no longer had to feel any responsibility to the Jews as God's Chosen People. This "Replacement Theology" would be exactly what would quiet the Church in Germany during World War II as the death camps sped into full swing. They had no obligation to the Jews. They [the Jews] were "suffering for their sins of rejecting the Messiah." It was as if Jesus' death cut them [the Church] free from these people rather than grafted them into their tree. However they saw it, it was this insidious virus—an invisible moderate anti-Semitism—that allowed the . . . Church to look the other way

as the most horrific and ungodly things were done.[153]

On the other hand, a 1923 article in the *Pentecostal Evangel* was quick to reassure its readers that the Jews would fulfill God's purpose for Israel—that the love of their homeland had been deeply instilled in the descendants of Abraham, Isaac, and Jacob; that their fervent prayer of "next year in Jerusalem" had echoed throughout the ages; and that God would hear that cry and respond. The article further assured that a tiny shoot of the fig tree was just beginning to break the soil in Palestine and nothing—not the Bishop of Jerusalem, not opposition from the Arabs, not replacement theology or those who were ignorant of God's Word—would hinder His plan for His Chosen People.[154]

Could it have been this belief that spurred Pope Paul IV to have a ghetto built in Rome? It was his papal decree, *Cum Nimis Absurdum*, issued in July 1555, which inflicted that indignity, as well as a plethora of other limitations and mortifications upon the Jews. Erected near the Tiber River, the ghetto, which the Jews were forced to finance, was prone to flooding and its gates were shut and locked after dark. As other leaders had done before—and since—Jews were forced to wear a yellow head covering as a means of identification.

Severe penalties were ordered for those Jews who disobeyed. In May 1998, Cardinal Edward Cassidy, representative of the Vatican Commission for Religious Relations with Jews, said that "the ghetto, which came into being in 1555 with a papal bull, became in Nazi Germany the antechamber of the extermination."[155]

Pope Pius IV, who assumed papal duties in 1559, provided a brief reprieve from some of the onerous edicts imposed by his predecessor, but that was short-lived. In 1566 his successor, Pius V, not only resurrected many of the decrees, but added even more arduous restrictions for the Jews. A mere three years later, the pope ordered the expulsion of Jews from his province. Three months later all Jews were forced out except for those in Rome and Ancona.

On the seesaw that is politics, Gregory XIII allowed them to return, but exacted severe restrictions. New prohibitions included not being allowed to drive carts and chariots in the streets; being forced to send members of their synagogue weekly to listen to Christian sermons; being force-fed and then made to race through the city during carnival; and being kept in prison for a certain length of time each year.

In 1585, Sixtus V relaxed the laws governing Jews in Europe, but that was soon negated by those who followed him: Clement VIII, Pius VI, and ultimately Pius IX. The seventeenth, eighteenth, and nineteenth centuries saw little change in the way Jews were treated. Martin Luther did achieve some reforms, but the Reformation did not change attitudes toward Jews of the Diaspora. They continued to be mocked, mistreated, and even murdered at the hands of their neighbors. The twentieth century with the rise of Nazism would prove to be the worst yet for the descendants of Abraham, Isaac, and Jacob.

ANIMOSITY BEGETS
ANTI-SEMITISM

AS A YOUNG CHILD, I learned about the pogroms in Russia from my Jewish mother when she told me of my great-grandfather, Mikel Katznelson. A rabbi in Minsk, he and his entire congregation were boarded up inside their synagogue on Shabbat and burned to death by Russian Orthodox Christians. As hungry flames consumed the structure, those gathered outside screamed, "Christ killers!" My relatives who were spared then fled Russia for what they thought would be a place of safety in Germany. Many who made that trek would later perish in Nazi concentration camps. My mother informed me, "Michael, Christians hate Jews; Christians kill Jews." It spurred me to become an advocate for and defender of the Jewish people.

The word *pogrom* is defined as:

> A violent riot aimed at the massacre or per-
> secution of an ethnic or religious group, par-
> ticularly one aimed at Jews. The term origi-
> nally entered the English language in order
> to describe 19th- and 20th-century attacks on
> Jews in the Russian Empire (mostly within
> the Pale of Settlement, what would become
> Ukraine and Belarus).[156]

The all-out attack was made even more horrific by beatings, murders, rapes, property destruction, and marauding
bands incited to plunder and burn the homes of Jews.
Pogroms were not limited to Russia, but spread into Austria,
the Balkan States, and eventually to Poland after 1918.

Following the assassination of Czar Alexander II in 1881,
false rumors spread naming Jews as the responsible parties.
Attacks against the Jews spread outward from the town of
Kirovograd, eventually reaching Kiev. For three long days
murderous mobs freely roamed the streets terrorizing the
Jewish inhabitants of the city—looting, destroying businesses
and homes, and leaving the wounded and dead in the streets.

Warsaw, Poland, was the site of deadly pogroms during
the celebrations of Christmas and Easter of that same year.

The results, no matter the cause, seemed to always be the same: Jews murdered, families burned out of their homes, and women raped. Pogroms would continue in some form to and beyond the turn of the century. In a few instances Russian leaders would attempt to stem the killing, but with little success. The deadly serpent of anti-Semitism would reemerge and homicidal hordes would again attack unsuspecting Jews.

As wave after wave of attacks rocked the Jewish communities of Eastern Europe, a mass exodus began to other countries, including the United States. It seemed that when any ill befell a village, town, or city, the finger was pointed at the Jews, and a horrible price was exacted. A pogrom that erupted in Kishinev during Passover in 1903 seized the attention of the world. In the aftermath of horror that flooded the town, forty-five Jews were slain and scores wounded. The savage murderers not only killed but mutilated the bodies of the dead.

Loath to sit back and wait for the axe to fall, a group of young men was organized to defend their fellow Jews. They were able to play a prominent role in saving lives and protecting property. Sadly, the group was unable to provide security for all the Jewish people who so desperately needed it.

In 1905 yet another, even more violent pogrom broke out in Odessa. The seed was planted in the early months of that year with charges that the Jews were not paying their fair share in the Russo-Japanese War. That accusation became the spark that erupted as a fire under the cauldron of Jew-hatred. On October 19, it had reached its boiling point as Russians by the hundreds gathered to exhibit their allegiance to Tsar Nicholas II. In the midst of the celebration, shots rang out. A young boy bearing an icon was killed. In his writing about anti-Semitic violence, Professor Robert Weinberg stated:

> To those residents of Odessa . . . Jews were a convenient and obvious target for retaliation. The legacy of discrimination against Russian Jewry and governmental tolerance and at times sponsorship of anti-Jewish organizations and propaganda provided fertile ground for a pogrom. When combined with economic resentments and frustrations, time-worn religious prejudices and the political polarization of Odessa society during 1905, the belief that Jews were revolutionaries and fears that they were prepared to use the

concessions of the manifesto as a springboard for the subjugation of non-Jews helped to create a situation fraught with frightening prospects. To those residents of Odessa alarmed by the opposition to the Tsar and government, Jews were a convenient and obvious target for retaliation.[157]

Richard Meinertzhagen, the son of a wealthy British banker, found himself in the midst of a pogrom in Odessa in 1910. He wrote:

> I have been shocked beyond belief. I have seldom been so angry . . . I witnessed a Pogrom in the streets of Odessa . . . Russians, many with bludgeons or knives or axes, were rushing all over the place, breaking open barricaded doors and chasing the wretched Jews into the streets where they were hunted down, beaten and often killed. . . . The climax arrived when a Russian passed the Consulate dragging a Jewish girl of about 12 years old by her hair along the gutter; she was screaming and the man was shouting. I have no doubt she would have been outraged

and then murdered. I could not help it . . . I dashed out, kicked the Russian violently in the stomach with my heavy Russian boots and landed him a good blow on the jaw; he went down like a log and I carried the child into the Consulate. . . .. I am deeply moved by these terrible deeds and have resolved that whenever or wherever I can help the Jews, I shall do so to the best of my ability.[158]

The fall of 1919 saw a resurgence of atrocities committed against the Jews by the White Army, a Russian counterrevolutionary group opposed to Leon Trotsky and his communist Red Army. Led by General Anton Denikin, the White Army declared war on the Jews beginning in September of that year in the town of Fastov. When the smoke had cleared and the screams were silenced, 1,500 Jewish men, women, and children had been slaughtered. These despicable deeds were not confined only to that small town, but spread into other regions, including Siberia and Belorussia.

Hannah Weiner, a twelve-year-old Jewish girl, wrote in her diary of the horror of the 1919 pogroms. Her daughter, Sheba Sweet, later published her mother's heartbreaking story of the times and the mobs who took to the streets:

Bands with names and without names. Altogether many in number. Ruthless beasts that marched upon towns to raid with joy and kill and destroy with laughter. God! What beastliness, what cruelty, what mad barbarism was perpetrated upon us and our brethren in those terrible days! Such utter bloodthirstiness, such mercilessness, such cruelty. To snicker and spit at a victim while torturing him to death! To bring a sword stained heavily with blood close to the nose of an old patriarch and ask him how he liked the odor and taste of Jewish blood! To ask him where is his God, and why doesn't he help him! . . . Torture that was worse than Death and hell itself.

I, as a child, ran loose around the streets with other children. And when I saw people in a bunch and crowded, sidled, pushed my way in, and stood breathlessly listening to the tales of horror.[159]

Nor was the White Army alone in its reprehensible treatment of Jews. As the opposing Red Army gained control

of the Ukraine, it joined the ranks of those wishing to annihilate the Jewish population. Entire towns and villages were
wiped out as communist troops marched across the land.
Many thought the worst had come upon the Jews' world,
but a bit over a decade later, the truth would be revealed in
all its reprehensible hatefulness as Adolf Hitler wormed his
way into power in Germany.

In actuality, Hitler had never been quiet regarding his
anti-Semitism, and his book *Mein Kampf* (My Struggle) spoke
eloquently about his hatred for the Jews, blaming them for
Communism among the other problems in the world. It is
said that Hitler could not go more than ten minutes without
talking about the Jews. Almost as soon as he took office,
laws went on the books barring Jews from government
employment, boycotting Jewish businesses, and restricting
their admission to universities. Hitler quoted from writings
by Martin Luther and Friedrich Nietzsche to support his
actions. This was the first test of how the nation would react
to Hitler's anti-Semitic legislation. According to German
historian Klaus Scholder: "during the decisive days around
the first of April [1933], no bishop, no church dignitaries, no
synod made any open declaration against the persecution
of the Jews in Germany."[160]

The silence of the German Church during this time is

one of the greatest indictments against Christianity in its entire history, but it also shows the incredible subtlety of the virus of anti-Semitism. One can be stricken with it and not even be aware of the infection; in reality, it had been active in the German culture for some time.

Even hero of the faith Dietrich Bonhoeffer seemed mildly infected, though he later became involved in trying to stop Hitler by conspiring to assassinate him, for which he was hung in 1945. He declared in regard to the 1933 boycott, "In the Church of Christ, we have never lost sight of the idea that the chosen people who nailed the Savior of the world to the Cross must bear the curse of the action through a long history of suffering."[161]

Some Christians did respond, however, but they were not living in Germany. Rees Howells, founder of The Bible College of Wales, a Christian Zionist, and fervent intercessor, encouraged his students to pray for the Jewish people. In September 1938, Howells heard that all the Jews had to leave Italy within six months, and that anti-Semitism was rapidly rising throughout Germany. He turned his thoughts toward the return of the Jews to their homeland. Rees Howells was one of hundreds, if not thousands, who were crying out to the world to allow the Jewish people a homeland.

Over the years, however, Nazi laws continued to become

increasingly harsh, as Jews were deprived of citizenship, systematically excluded from employment, forbidden to own cars, banned from attending public schools, and stripped of their property.[162] At first, the idea was to drive all Jews out of Germany so that the country would become *Judenrein*, or "free of Jews."

Most of the German Jews, however, were reluctant to leave, but events escalated to new heights on November 9, 1938, when mobs turned on the Jews after fabricated reports that a young Jew had assassinated a German official in Paris. During the *Kristallnacht* ("Night of Broken Glass") dozens of Jews were killed in riots, windows of Jewish shops and homes were smashed, and synagogues were set afire. Thousands of Jews were arrested.

When Germany invaded Poland in 1939, the two million Jews there were subject to even harsher laws as they were forced into ghettos surrounded by walls and barbed wire. During the Nazis' invasion of the Soviet Union in June of 1941, special units called *Einsatzgruppen* ("action squads") were dispatched to kill Jews on sight. Before long, rumors of the killings were circulating in capitals around the world. Orders had already been issued by second-in-command Hermann Göring to make ready for the Nazis' "final solution to the Jewish question." In September of 1941 Russian Jews were already being forced to wear the yellow six-pointed star that distinguished them from Aryans, and in the following months tens of thousands were deported to the ghettos of Poland. Only months before, in November 1940, when American Jews in France were forced the wear the stars, the United States protested but received no response from Germany. Regrettably, American leaders said and did nothing.

The Lodz Ghetto was the second largest established by the Nazis. There were several additional cities in which Jews were forced to reside inside fenced areas: Warsaw, Krakow, Bialystok, Czestochowa, Kielce, Lublin, Lvóv, Radom, and Vilna. Some of the compounds held as many as 400,000 (Warsaw), and some as few as 3,000 and were only gathering places for Jews until they could be transported to larger ghettos.

February 1940 was the beginning of the end for most of the 160,000 Jewish residents of Lodz. With little warning, they were rounded up by German troops and forced into an area approximately 4.3 square kilometers (a bit more than 1.5 square miles). The perimeter was outlined with barbed wire and was patrolled by units of special police. Conditions inside the ghetto were abominable—little food, no running water, the absence of a sewer system, which exacerbated disease. That environment was heightened by forced labor, overpopulation, and hunger. Death stalked the streets of the ghetto. A child, Pavel Friedman, confined in Terezin wrote a graphic and heartbreaking poem, "I Never Saw Another Butterfly." It speaks so eloquently of being separated from the outside world:

> For seven weeks I've lived in here,
>
> Penned up inside this ghetto.
>
> But I have found what I love here.
>
> The dandelions call to me
>
> And the white chestnut branches in the court.
>
> Only I never saw another butterfly.
>
> That butterfly was the last one.
>
> Butterflies don't live in here, in the ghetto.[163]

In that same month, the gassing vans—trucks that would seal and suffocate those in it with carbon monoxide gas—began being employed. These were eventually replaced by the first of the death camps, Chelmno, which opened in late 1941. After the death camp operations were activated, full-scale deportation from the ghettos to the camps was inaugurated. The heaviest deportations took place in the summer and fall of 1942.[164] By the time Soviet troops reached the Lodz ghetto on January 19, 1945, there remained only 877 Jews; over 245,000 had been held captive from its inception in 1939.

There appears little doubt that the United States knew of Hitler's oppression in these early years, though at the time there were no known plans in Germany for the "final solution." The US ambassador to Germany whom Roosevelt replaced with William E. Dodd warned the Germans that there would be an ill reception in the United States if the Nazi government took to mistreating the Jews. It took Dodd himself less than a year to see that he was dealing with a government filled with unscrupulous men. "It was definitely the aim of the [Nazi] government . . . to eliminate the Jews from German life," one State Department officer wrote. By 1937 it was clear that the Nazi persecution was systematic and progressing toward an unfathomable end. Conditions were made as uncomfortable as possible for the Jews who chose to stay in Germany. Although tens of thousands left the country, there were still millions who stayed. The problem was that other nations refused the Jews entrance even if they did desire to leave. The doors were slowly closing to European Jews everywhere; and by 1939, they were basically shut. For the U.S., the "Great Door" period of welcoming the world to its shores was over.

HITLER'S "JUSTIFICATION"

THE JEWS, both in Europe and Asia, were denigrated, shunned, forced into baptism upon threat of death, burned alive in their synagogues, refused medical and legal aid, stripped of their businesses and material possessions, and finally all but exterminated. The Nazis were not responsible for the invention of anti-Semitism in its vilest forms; they merely built on the foundation laid down through the centuries preceding the events of the twentieth century.

A few centuries after Luther's Ninety-five Theses were nailed to the doors of the cathedral in Wittenberg, a madman would arise from among the masses and declare that Jews were responsible for all of Germany's economic ills. Or perhaps Adolf Hitler had read the works of philosopher Houston Stewart Chamberlain, who wrote in a letter to his Aunt Harriet that Germany was "menaced by complete moral and intellectual ruin if a strong reaction does not set in against the supremacy of the Jews, who feed upon them and suck—at every grade of society—their very little blood."[165]

This same mindset would plague the church well into the twentieth century. In 1922, Hitler declared the Jewish people to be Germany's No. 1 enemy, the race accountable for all the nation's internal problems. He strongly stressed what he saw as "the anti-Semitism of reason" that must lead "to the systematic combating and elimination of Jewish privileges. Its ultimate goal must implacably be the total removal of the Jews."[166] He was so convinced Germany was near collapse, that he joined forces with nationalist leader General Erich Friedrich Wilhelm Ludendorff in an attempted coup.

The ensuing riot that began in a Munich beer hall resulted in: 1) the deaths of sixteen individuals, 2) the Nazi Party being outlawed, and 3) Hitler being tried and sentenced to five years in prison. His sentence was commuted to nine months; during his incarceration, he dictated a draft of *Mein Kampf* to Rudolf Hess, a devoted sycophant. This tome, filled with a coarse, ill-conceived jumble of anti-Semitism, fabrication, and fantasy, evolved into the literal bible of the emerging Nazi Party. By 1939, this paean of pretense had sold five million volumes and had been translated into eleven languages.

It was also in 1922 that Hitler fully outlined his plan in a conversation with a friend, appropriately named Joseph Hell:

> If I am ever really in power, the destruction of the Jews will be my first and most important job. As soon as I have power, I shall have gallows after gallows erected, for example, in Munich on the Marienplatz—as many of them as traffic allows. Then the Jews will be hanged one after another, and they will stay hanging until they stink. They will stay hanging as long as hygienically possible. As soon as they are untied, then the next group will follow and that will continue until the last Jew in Munich is exterminated. Exactly the same procedure will be followed in other cities until Germany is cleansed of the last Jew![167]

Philosopher Chamberlain wrote to encourage Hitler in a letter dated October 7, 1923. He zealously advised the führer that he was perceived as the "opposite of a politician . . . for the essence of all politics is membership of a party, whereas with you all parties disappear, consumed by the heat of your love for the fatherland."[168] In a later missive to Hitler, Chamberlain asserted:

> One cannot simultaneously embrace Jesus and those who crucified him. This is the splendid thing about Hitler—his courage. In this respect he reminds one of [Martin] Luther.[169]

It is quite obvious from his writings that Chamberlain also viewed Jewish industrialists as Germany's "public enemy No. 1."

The German ruling class made what proved to be a disastrous error in judgment in 1925 by removing prohibitions against the Nazi Party and granting permission for Hitler to address the public. Moreover, when he needed it most in order to expand the reach of the party, a worldwide economic crisis enveloped Germany. Ironically, the resulting magnitude of unemployment, panic, and anger afforded Hitler the opportunity to step forward and claim the role of redeemer and savior of the nation. On January 30, 1933, Weimar Republic of Germany President Paul von Hindenburg was persuaded to nominate Hitler as Reich chancellor. Germany had lost its last chance to avoid a Second World War—and the Holocaust.

Hitler's determination to outfox his opponents and remove conservatives from any role in the government took little time or effort. He abolished free trade unions, removed Communists, Social Democrats, and Jews from any participation in politics, and consigned his rivals to concentration camps. He solidified his hold on Germany in March 1933 with the use of persuasive argument, indoctrination, fear, and coercion. The façade was firmly in place, and the people of Germany were soon intimidated into subjugation.

With the death of von Hindenburg in August of 1934, the Third Reich had a determined dictator who held the reins both of führer (leader) and chancellor, as well as all the powers accorded to a head of state. He abandoned the Treaty of Versailles, conscripted a massive army, supplied it with war materiel, and in 1938 forced the British and French into signing the Munich Agreement. Soon to follow were laws against Jews, the construction of concentration camps, the destruction of the state of Czechoslovakia, the invasion of Poland, and a soon-to-be-broken nonaggression pact with the USSR. The only obstacles standing between Hitler and the rest of the world were US president Franklin D. Roosevelt, British Prime Minister Winston Churchill, general secretary of the Central Committee of the Communist

Party of the Soviet Union Joseph Stalin, and the armies of Western civilization.

Just one week after Roosevelt was sworn into office for his initial term as chief executive, German laborers had completed Dachau, the original concentration camp. Within its confines some 40,000 individuals would be murdered, most of them Jews. Hitler followed the opening of the camp by nationalizing the Gestapo (secret police) and bringing it under his full control. Just three months later, he had successfully combined all commands under the aegis of the Nazi Party.

Reinhold Niebuhr, an early Zionist and liberal son whose German-born father was pastor of a German Evangelical Synod flock in Illinois (now part of the United Church of Christ) preached against what he called "Jewish bigotry" among fellow Christians. In 1933, he tried to warn believers about Hitler's "cultural annihilation of the Jews."[170] He stated, "The fact is that the Nazis have a new mythology in which the Jew is cast as the role of a devil."[171]

Niebuhr was one of the few Protestant leaders who tried to turn attention to the rising tide of anti-Semitism that was slowly inundating Nazi Germany. At first he was disbelieving, but by 1938, he could no longer bury his head in the sand. As Hitler's troops marched into Vienna, Niebuhr was confident that "the ultimate in man's sadistic tendencies"[172] had been revealed.

A turning point for many Jews in Germany was reached on November 9, 1938, a night that lives in the bitter memory of millions of Jews as the aforementioned *Kristallnacht,* so named because of the sound of shattered glass as Jewish shops in Germany were destroyed by Hitler's storm troopers. More than 260 synagogues were burned that night and 20,000 Jews were arrested. Incredibly, the Jewish community was then fined $400 million for damages inflicted by the soldiers to their property. From that moment on, Adolf Hitler began to speak openly of annihilating the Jews. It was difficult for anyone to bury their heads in the sand and ignore what was happening to their Jewish neighbors. The White Paper of 1939 condemned millions of European Jews to the concentration camps.

Niebuhr's contempt for Lutheran Church members in Nazi Germany, whose "hasty capitulation to the Nazi racial doctrines"[173] he found inexcusable, was outdistanced only by his contempt for the German Roman Catholic Church. He rather unflatteringly described the lackadaisical attitude of the Church as having been "reduced to the pathetic role of begging the Nazis kindly to let it cooperate in their anti-Communist campaign."[174]

Meanwhile, the British Mandate ended amid the degradation, mutilations, and deaths of the Holocaust. Six million Jews were slaughtered in Hitler's death camps and gas chambers. For the most part and for whatever reasons, European Christians remained silent under the glare of Nazi intimidation.

How is this relevant today? Too often world leaders remain silent as Israel is castigated and censured for fear of being cut off by petroleum-producing Arab countries. Moral and spiritual values have been forced to bow to the idol of Black Gold.

In 1935, the Nuremberg Laws were instituted and German Jews lost their citizenship with its rights and privileges. They were then totally under the cruel fist of Hitler and his rabid Jew-hatred. Like many of the Jews in the earlier days of Hitler's rule, Roosevelt, too, was deceived by the picture presented to the world at the 1936 Olympics. American historian and author Deborah Lipstadt wrote:

> The sports competition was a massive exercise in propaganda and public relations, and many American reporters were uncritical about all that they saw. . . . Americans, particularly non-German speaking ones who only

knew Germany from the Games—departed convinced that the revolutionary upheavals, random beatings, and the murders of political opponents had been greatly exaggerated or were a thing of the past. Those bedazzled included not only the athletes and tourists, but personages such as newspaper publisher Norman Chandler and numerous American businessmen. This period marked the beginning of Charles Lindbergh's love affair with the Reich. One reporter was convinced that as a result of the Games visitors would be . . . inclined to dismiss all anti-German thought and action abroad as insipid and unjust. [The visitor] sees no Jewish heads being chopped off, or even roundly cudgeled. . . . The people smile, are polite, and sing with gusto at the beer gardens. Visitors to Berlin described it as a warm, hospitable place and Germany as a country well on its way to solving the economic and unemployment problems which still plagued America.[175]

While Hitler was making plans to wreak havoc in

Europe, the Jewish community in 1938 Jerusalem was trying to persuade the British to increase immigration quotas. The British, however, saw increased allotments only as putting a match to the Arab fuse—a short one, at that. So we read the agonizing accounts of Jewish refugees strikingly similar to the Spanish Jews during Columbus' time. But now many were struggling to escape Hitler's iron fist only to perish in the waters of the Mediterranean in unseaworthy ships that could find no safe harbor.

As events of the mid-to-late 1930s led ominously toward a Second World War, the Nazis under Hitler had already been searching for a "final solution" for what they considered the Jewish problem.

After years of this continuous rhetoric, it took ninety minutes for Adolf Hitler's henchmen to determine the fate of six million Jews. During that period, the Holocaust became a heinous reality when on January 20, 1942, Hitler's architects of death met at the beautiful Wannsee Villa located in a serene lakeside suburb of Berlin. Their stated objective was to find a "Final Solution to the Jewish Question."

Presiding over the conference was SS-Lieutenant General Reinhard Heydrich, chief of the Security Police and Security Service. As the meeting began, Heydrich was determined that none should doubt his superiority or his authority, which was not limited by geographical borders. He briefed those in the room on measures that had already been taken against the Jews in the attempt to eradicate them from both the German culture and homeland.

In attendance were fourteen high-ranking German military and government leaders, among them Adolf Eichmann. Over a ninety-minute luncheon, fifteen men changed the world forever. January 20, 2012, marked the 70th anniversary of that fateful conference. We dare not let these dubious anniversaries pass without marking how little time it takes to alter the course of history.

Initially, steps had been implemented to allow German Jews to immigrate to whatever countries would accept them, but the move proved to be too slow for the führer and the Reich. Now the men gathered to implement Hitler's new solution. Heydrich provided a list of the number of Jews in each country; a total of eleven million Jews were to be involved. In his zeal he determined:

> In large, single-sex labor columns, Jews fit to work will work their way eastward constructing roads. Doubtless, the large majority will be eliminated by natural causes. Any final remnant that survives will doubtless consist

of the most resistant elements. They will have
to be dealt with appropriately because otherwise, by natural selection, they would form
the germ cell of a new Jewish revival.[176]

Translation: All must die.

According to the minutes of the meeting, Jews were to
be purged, beginning in Germany, Bohemia, and Moravia.
After that, they were to be expunged in Europe from east
to west. Many questions arose as to how to identify those
considered to be Jews. This issue was not resolved during
the Wannsee meeting, but would be brutally dealt with later.

Of course, it was not the beginning of the extermination
of the Jewish people. Many of the Nazi elite in attendance
had already participated in mass murders since the summer
of 1941. Even before the gathering at Wannsee, more than a
half million Jews had been executed behind army lines. The
question was how to attain the goal of total extermination in
areas outside the battle zone. A more efficient way needed to
be found to eliminate larger numbers. No, the meeting was
not called to determine how to begin the process but rather
to spell out how the "final solution" would be achieved. By
January, death camps equipped with gas chambers and
ovens were under construction.

The ordinary citizenry of Germany did not enter the war determined to annihilate six million of their neighbors. It began with a subversive program of anti-Semitism aimed at blaming the Jewish people for all the ills that had beset Germany following its losses in World War I. Perhaps even Hitler did not begin with total extermination in mind. That seed probably began to germinate only after he realized that Jews were denied entry into other countries. It seemed to Hitler, then, that he had been given a green light to do whatever he wished with the Jewish population. Ultimately, his "final solution" was the Holocaust—the deaths of six million Jewish men, women, and children murdered in the most horrific of ways.

ANTI-SEMITISM: ALIVE AND GROWING

WHILE JEW-HATRED in Arab states is to be expected, in Europe it is not just a thing of the past—a product of the Nazis and the Holocaust. In the past decade, it has become more blatant and deliberate. In April 2011, a synagogue on the Greek Island of Corfu was burned. What was the threat on this idyllic island? A mere one hundred fifty Jews. Unfortunately, this was not an isolated incident. Jewish synagogues in France, Sweden, Hungary, and Poland have been vandalized or burned and with cemeteries desecrated. Jewish men have had to resort to wearing hats or caps in order to hide their *yarmulkes* and escape harassment. Schools have been forced to erect iron gates and hire security to protect Jewish children. In Malmo, Sweden, the population of Jews has decreased from 2,000 to less than 700 in recent years because of threats of violence—inflicted or perceived.

Death threats against those who would dare defend Israel have become commonplace today, and when university professors are allowed to lecture on the topic of Israel, protests often turn violent.

Felix Frankfurter, emeritus professor at Harvard Law School, and later Associate Justice of the Supreme Court, provided an example of this attempt at campus censorship:

> These current manifestations of a widespread culture of victimization and grievance are only the most recent iterations of a dangerous long-term trend on campuses both in the United States and in Europe. The ultimate victims are freedom of expression, academic freedom and the free exchange of ideas. . . . The groups demanding censorship of my lecture included Hopkins Feminists, Black Student Union, Diverse Sexuality and General Alliance, Sexual Assault Resource Unit and Voice for Choice. I have been told that two faculty members urged these students, who had never heard of me, to organize

the protests, but the cowardly faculty members would not themselves sign the petition. The petition contained blatant lies about me and my views, but that is beside the point. I responded to the lies in my lecture and invited the protesting students to engage me during the Q and A. But instead, they walked out in the middle of my presentation, while I was discussing the prospects for peace in the Mid-East. . . . According to the Johns Hopkins News-Letter, another petition claimed that "by denying Israel's alleged war crimes against Palestinians" I violated the university's "anti-harassment policy" and its "statement of ethical standards." In other words, by expressing my reasonable views on a controversial subject, I harassed students.[177]

The anti-Semitism of Hitler's Europe seemed to sharply abate following the war, but has returned with a vengeance. The counterfeit and duplicitous book *The Protocols of the Learned Elders of Zion* is widely available in Muslim bookstores throughout Europe, and it has generated a renewed fascination in the Jews as scapegoats for the world's ills. This is exacerbated, as it was in World War II Germany, by rising economic worries. The demonization of the Jewish State of Israel by Muslims worldwide has been adopted by many Europeans, adding to the growth of Jew-hatred.

Those seeking a peaceful coexistence with Muslim immigrants are finding it easier to join in the anti-Semitic fray than to stand for Israel's right to exist. This is hypocrisy at its best . . . or worst. In an attempt to bypass negotiations with Israel for a two-state solution in the Middle East, Mahmoud Abbas, the current Palestinian Authority president, devised a plan to declare unilateral statehood. For months, he traversed the globe to meet with leaders of various countries in attempts to garner support for a UN vote that would declare a Palestinian state. A simple majority vote by the General Assembly in 2011 would have conferred permanent observer status on the Palestinian Authority. Abbas could then have sought full-member status from the Security Council. (On November 29, 2012, Abbas realized his vision; the Palestinian Authority was granted UN Observer State status.)

In his UN General Assembly speech on September 22, 2011, French president Nicholas Sarkozy challenged US efforts to halt a Palestinian attempt to declare a unilateral state without negotiations with Israel by saying: "Let us cease our endless debates on the parameters to observer status. Let us begin negotiations, and adopt a precise timetable."[178]

Oil-rich Middle Eastern states—the last bastion of family-run corporations erroneously called countries—terrified by undercurrents of seething internal rebellion, have decided to play the "J" card. The perfect stick with which to stir the pot is the Palestinian issue. These corrupt regimes hope to shift the focus from injustices done to their own people onto the Jews—and the Jews present the perfect scapegoat, just as they did when Hitler wrested power.

In September 2001, just seventy-two hours before the two attacks on the World Trade Center, a third on the Pentagon, and the fourth at an unknown target in the nation's capital that was aborted, the UN hosted Durban I in South Africa. At that conference Zionism was proclaimed to be racism, and Israel was declared an apartheid state. The Jews were accused of controlling the world, its banks, its wars, and of having invented many of the major diseases—including AIDS. It was another shameful display of anti-Semitism.

Has it been so long ago that people have forgotten the origins of the PLO, which now hides under the banner of the Palestinian Authority? This organization, whose leader is demanding unilateral statehood, was responsible for the Munich massacre during the 1972 Summer Olympics. Its chief financial officer at that time was Abu Mazen (a.k.a. the afore-mentioned Mahmoud Abbas). It has, over the years, been equally complicit in hijacking airplanes (TWA, Pan-Am, and BOAC), attacking school buses filled with Jewish children, and murdering, maiming, and mutilating the innocent. Its members have killed Americans abroad: ambassador to the Sudan Cleo Noel, his Charge d'Affairs George Curtis Moore, and Leon Klinghoffer, a wheelchair-bound Jewish invalid, aboard the AchilleLauro cruise ship, to name just three of the many victims of the PLO.

Terrorist groups embedded within the lands of the Palestinian Authority have been responsible for numerous heinous and deadly attacks inside Israel: car bombs; backpacks laden with explosives, ball bearings, screws, nails, and other deadly projectiles; sneak attacks on unsuspecting families; and more. Ready acceptance of terrorism and anti-Semitism has become just as much a part of the human psyche as death and taxes. And yet, as a writer for the *Pentecostal Evangel* reminded: "No nation ever lost anything by treating the Jews with kindness . . . No nation ever gained by persecuting that nation."[179]

Hitler came to believe that before he could begin his campaign to eradicate the Jewish population, he had to desensitize the German population by blaming the Jews.

This is why *The Protocols* was required reading in every school in Germany at that time.

A word of warning: Some of today's rhetoric printed by the Liberal Left media in support of terrorists is chillingly reminiscent of propaganda that flooded Nazi Germany during World War II, written by Hitler himself. Some examples:

> We are putting an end to the wrong path mankind has taken. . . . Conscience is a Jewish invention. Like circumcision, it mutilates man. . . . There is no such thing as truth, either in the moral or in the scientific sense. . . . One must distrust mind and conscience; one must place one's trust in one's instincts.[180]

Roman Catholic theologian and advocate of Jewish–Catholic reconciliation, Monsignor John M. Oesterreicher, wrote of Hitler's diabolical plan to blame the Jews:

> Apparently, several motives spurred Hitler and his cohorts. The most obvious was a tactical one: Agitation against the Jews was a "superb" means of propaganda, a political and economic weapon in Germany as well as in the occupied countries. By pointing to

a secret enemy, the Nazis thought to distract attention from their own doings. While they railed against "a Jewish plot for world domination," they had their followers sing: "Today Germany is ours, tomorrow the entire world." . . . Though it became carefully planned strategy, its roots lay not in the calculating mind but in more primitive reactions. For the most part, the Nazis were hollow men who craved an ideology that would save them from their inner emptiness; they were misfits who needed the illusion of grandeur. Rather than watch their own disintegration, they let instinct push them toward the destruction of others. . . . It was Jewry, Hitler declared again and again, that sought to encircle Germany, ruin it economically, and enslave it politically. It was the Jews who directed British imperialism, American plutocracy, and Russian bolshevism.[181]

Pew Research Center reported in a 2013 study that "harassment of Jews had reached a seven-year high." And furthermore: "In Europe, for example, Jews were harassed by individuals or social groups in 34 of the region's 45 countries."[182]

Following the 2015 attack on the French magazine *Charlie Hebdo* that left twelve journalists dead and at least eleven injured—four critically, a single jihadist burst through the front doors of Hyper Cacher, a kosher supermarket in Porte de Vincennes in eastern Paris. Before the smell of gunpowder had dissipated and the gunman killed, four hostages had died a brutal and terrifying death.

Some leaders in France have reported that vitriolic, anti-Jewish speech has escalated in recent years, as has the stigma against anti-Semitism. Jews in the area attribute some of that upswing to men such as French-Cameroonian actor Dieudonné. During his sold-out, one-man performances, the entertainer cracks offensive jokes about the Holocaust. Had those same jokes been made about Islam or the Prophet Mohammad, the outcome would almost certainly have been much different, as demonstrated by the *Charlie Hebdo* attack. Of course, Jews suggested that increased attacks on targets such as cemeteries, synagogues, supermarkets, and pharmacies—accompanied by shouts of "death to Jews"—would eventually lead to a more violent assault. They were correct.

The difference between today's assaults and the Holocaust is that there has not yet arisen a singular personage to lead the charge against Europe's Jews. Yet, slowly but surely, the religious freedoms that have been enjoyed by the Jewish people since the end of World War II are eroding. The question must be: Will the church respond differently than it did during the Holocaust, when there was hardly any response at all? Will believers stand with Israel and the Jewish people, or will many turn their backs out of fear?

In 1984 a group in Britain began monitoring anti-Semitic attacks against Jews. The organization reported twice as many incidents in 2014 as there had been the previous year. The more egregious of the assaults was against Jewish schoolchildren, and worshipers entering or leaving synagogues.

Lest one think anti-Semitism is confined to Europe or the Middle East, that myth is exposed in the comments of a Democratic congressman from the state of Georgia. In reference to the push for a two-state division of Israel, Representative Hank Johnson pronounced:

> There has been a steady [stream], almost like termites can get into a residence and eat before you know that you've been eaten up and you fall in on yourself, there has been settlement activity that has marched forward

with impunity and at an ever increasing rate to the point where it has become alarming.

That discourse was quickly followed by an apology—not for his appalling rhetoric, but for his "choice of words."[183]

One might think that following the Holocaust, the world would unite to halt anti-Semitic attacks wherever they might be found. Not so! One poll indicated that as many as one of every four European citizens harbors some form of Jew-hatred. That figure alone should reveal that not enough is being done to change attitudes and combat the menace that is as old as time.

Perhaps an article that first appeared in *U.S. News and World Report* conveys it best:

It is time for people of all beliefs and nationalities to stand together against anti-Semitism and all forms of intolerance and hatred.[184]

RECONCILIATION
OR CHANGE

THE STUDY OF HISTORY is a worthwhile endeavor. Why? George Santayana wrote, "Those who do not remember the past are condemned to repeat it."[185] Delving into the history of the church will lead to a better understanding of who we are and what we believe, of the events that have fashioned the church today, and will provide insight into what we need to do in order to make crucial course adjustments. The author of *The Message* paints a vivid picture of what can happen if we fail to heed the lessons of history:

> Remember our history, friends, and be
> warned. All our ancestors were led by the

providential Cloud and taken miraculously through the Sea. They went through the waters, in a baptism like ours, as Moses led them from enslaving death to salvation life. They all ate and drank identical food and drink, meals provided daily by God. They drank from the Rock, God's fountain for them that stayed with them wherever they were. And the Rock was Christ. But just experiencing God's wonder and grace didn't seem to mean much—most of them were defeated by temptation during the hard times in the desert, and God was not pleased.

The same thing could happen to us. We must be on guard so that we never get caught up in wanting our own way as they did. And we must not turn our religion into a circus as they did—"First the people partied, then they threw a dance." We must not be sexually promiscuous—they paid for that, remember, with 23,000 deaths in one day! We must never try to get Christ to serve us instead of us serving him; they tried it, and God launched an epidemic of poisonous snakes. We must be careful not to stir up discontent; discontent destroyed them.

These are all warning markers—DANGER!— in our history books, written down so that we don't repeat their mistakes. Our positions in the story are parallel—they at the beginning, we at the end—and we are just as capable of messing it up as they were. Don't be so naive and self-confident. You're not exempt. You could fall flat on your face as easily as anyone else. Forget about self-confidence; it's useless. Cultivate God-confidence. (I Corinthians 10:1–12)

Students of religion might read the accounts of Constantine and his ventures and of the Crusaders and their battles, drawing only the conclusion that the church was consumed with the pursuit of violent endeavors. Upon further study, it would be discovered that Constantine elevated the early church from torture and suffering to an entirely new status in Rome. The Crusades were launched during a period when papal politics were driven by the passion of greed. Nothing about the Crusades was based on grace or love for one's fellowman.

It is easy to look back at those times and wonder how the church could have gotten so far off course as to involve itself in the initiation of wars. We seem to forget that it is the work of the "Father of Lies" to dispense heresy and to turn the weird and wacky into sometimes acceptable religious beliefs. Examining the church from its inception on the Day of Pentecost down through the ages provides needed insight allowing us to sever the ridiculous from the sublime, the sacrilege from the sacred.

The early church was given unprecedented insight. Its leaders had walked closely with Jesus. They had heard firsthand His words in John 14:6 (ESV):

> Jesus said to him, "I am the way, and the truth, and the life. No one comes to the Father except through me."

The disciples and many of Jesus' followers had been present when He healed the sick, caused the lame to leap with joy, turned water into wine, surveyed a field filled with 5,000 hungry people and fed them all. They heard Him forgive sins and teach the way of love, grace, and forgiveness. Those men and women knew that when Jesus said, "I am the WAY," He wasn't being arrogant or egotistical—and neither were they when they repeated His assertions. They had been in His presence and "tasted" that the Lord was good (Psalm 34:8).

Christianity, as practiced by the early church, was first and foremost a relationship, not a philosophy or a religion. It was not about who could build the most elaborate and ostentatious cathedrals. It was not about who could preach the showiest of sermons, or who could establish the best and most demanding rituals. It was not about programs, procedures, performances, or personages. It was simply the story of Jesus Christ, the babe born of a virgin; the Son of God and the Son of Man willing to die to erase the sins of the world.

Christ's early disciples were more concerned with spreading the unadulterated gospel, not the watered-down version so often seen today. The result was, "And the Lord added to the church daily those who were being saved" (Acts 2:47 NKJV).

The great orator C. H. Spurgeon preached a sermon on April 5, 1874, titled "Building the Church." He outlined four points garnered from Acts 2:42–47:

"They devoted themselves to the apostles' teaching and to the fellowship, to the breaking of bread and to prayer."

In the apostle's teaching. They were a doctrinal church, they believed in being devoted to the unmovable truth; they did not belong to the shifty generation of men who plead that their views are progressive, and that they cannot hold themselves bound by [an] ordinary creed. Dear brothers and sisters, never give up the grand old truths of the gospel. . . .

Next they were devoted in fellowship. They loved each other, and they continued doing so. They conversed with one another about the things of God, and they did not give up the conversation. They helped each other when they were in need, and they continued in such kindness. . . .

Next they continued in the breaking of bread, which is a delightful ordinance, and never to be despised or underestimated. As often as they could they celebrated the death of Christ, until he would come again. . . .

They also remained devoted in prayer. Mark that! God cannot bless a church which does not pray, and churches must increase in supplication if they would increase in strength.[186]

So powerful, so refreshing, and so meaningful was the message of Jesus that people were drawn from darkness into His light. John wrote in chapter 1, verse 4, "In Him was life, and the life was the light of men" (NKJV). The early church was filled with people who were eager and enthusiastic followers of Christ. Many churches today—many Christians today—have lost that excitement. They resemble the parable of the sower in Luke 8:14: "Now the ones that fell among thorns are those who, when they have heard, go out and are choked with cares, riches, and pleasures of life, and bring no fruit to maturity" (NKJV).

The church today is an amalgamation of evolution rather than the simple biblical teachings of the New Testament Church. Today, breaking of bread together in celebration of the Last Supper has become only a ritual rather than the observance it was meant to be. The Lord's Supper is symbolic of the relationship between Jesus and His followers; and it is also a promise of an event to come. Jesus said, "Truly I tell you, I will not drink again from the fruit of the vine until that day when I drink it new in the kingdom of God" (Mark 14:25 NIV). Witnessing to the lost has become rote rather than a joyful sharing of the change Christ has made in a life. Do we tick off all the boxes? Did we repeat the steps in perfect order? Did we really sell the product? How do we close the deal and add another notch to our "gospel gun"? Believers are called to be witnesses and not supersalesmen, a concept that holds many back for fear of failure.

Church leadership has devolved from a role of servant-hood to one of a professional administrator. Has the role of servant become all too absent from the church today? In Mark 9:33–35 (MSG), Jesus gathered the disciples around Him in Capernaum. He asked:

> "What were you discussing on the road?" The silence was deafening—they had been arguing with one another over who among them was greatest. He sat down and summoned the Twelve. "So you want first place? Then take the last place. Be the servant of all."

After Martin Luther nailed the Ninety-five Theses to the door of the cathedral, the Protestant movement began to grow. The website "Religion Facts" provides information into the initial divisions:

As the Reformation developed in Germany, various groups in other parts of Europe also began to break away from the Catholic Church. Reformed Christianity developed in Switzerland based on the teachings of Ulrich Zwingli and John Calvin. When it spread to Scotland under John Knox, the Reformed faith became Presbyterianism. Switzerland was also the birthplace of the Anabaptists, spiritual ancestors of today's Amish, Mennonites, Quakers, and Baptists. Anglicanism was established in 1534 when England's King Henry VIII broke from the authority of the Pope, and became Episcopalianism in America. Methodism, based on the teachings of John Wesley, also has its roots in Anglicanism.[187]

Through the years there have been other divisions from these denominations, such as the Pentecostal and Charismatic churches. Today we are faced with an incomprehensible selection of a most perplexing variety. The tendency is to wring our hands and, as did Elijah the prophet, declare, "I alone am left; and they seek to take my life" (1 Kings 19:14

NKJV). God quickly corrected that fallacy in verse 18: "Yet I have reserved seven thousand in Israel, all whose knees have not bowed to Baal, and every mouth that has not kissed him." In words for the church today, "God has a faithful remnant that will not be shaken—pastors, missionaries, men, women, and children—who love Him and, as David wrote in Psalm 63:8, "follows close behind" Him (NKJV).

The early church fell prey to the overindulgences established by King Constantine and exacerbated by many of the church leaders that followed. The Reformation was to be a break from some of those excesses, but as decade followed decade and century followed century, we began to see the development of a church driven in some instances by relativism, expediency, and materialism. Author Chris Armstrong suggested:

> "Many 20- and 30-something evangelicals are uneasy and alienated in mall-like church environments; high-energy, entertainment-oriented worship; and boomer-era ministry strategies and structures modeled on the business world. Increasingly, they are asking just how these culturally camouflaged churches can help them rise above the values of the

consumerist world around them." Such young people yearn for calls to spiritual discipline, commitment, sacrifice, and selfless service.[188]

This battle can be won through moral clarity and the power or prayer. Yes, America must be willing to face radical Islam militarily, but the "heavy lifting" must be done by believers engaged in "effective, fervent prayer" (see James 5:16).

The writer of Hebrews reminds us:

> These people all trusted God and as a result won battles, overthrew kingdoms, ruled their people well, and received what God had promised them; they were kept from harm in a den of lions and in a fiery furnace. Some, through their faith, escaped death by the sword. Some were made strong again after they had been weak or sick. Others were given great power in battle; they made whole armies turn and run away. (Hebrews 11:33–34 TLB)

The psalmist also encourages the believer:

> God is our refuge and strength, a tested

help in times of trouble. And so we need not
fear even if the world blows up and the mountains crumble into the sea. Let the oceans
roar and foam; let the mountains tremble!
(Psalm 46:1–3 TLB)

The battle for the kind of church for which God longs
cannot be won if we sleep. This is a war between light and
darkness. Let me remind you again what the prophet Ezekiel
said:

But if the watchman sees the sword
coming and does not blow the trumpet, and
the people are not warned, and the sword
comes and takes any person from among
them, he is taken away in his iniquity; but
his blood I will require at the watchman's
hand. (Ezekiel 33:6 NKJV)

Isaiah wrote:

I have set watchmen on your walls, O Jerusalem;
They shall never hold their peace day or night.
You who make mention of the LORD, do not
    keep silent,
And give Him no rest till He establishes

And till He makes Jerusalem a praise

in the earth. (Isaiah 62:6–7 NKJV)

The apostle Paul stated:

Now the Lord is the Spirit; and where the

Spirit of the Lord is, there is liberty. (2 Cor-

inthians 3:17 NKJV)

When God's Spirit is present, there is liberty and freedom. When the Spirit is present, there is dominion. It is time for the church of the living God to arise. Jonathan Stockstill wrote "Let the Church Rise." The chorus of the song reminds us:

Let the Church rise from the ashes

Let the Church fall to her knees

Let us be light in the darkness

Let the Church rise.

The Good News today is that God still moves through His Holy Spirit! I leave you with these scriptures:

At that time Michael shall stand up, the

great prince who stands watch over the sons

of your people; and there shall be a time of

trouble, such as never was since there was

a nation, even to that time. And at that time your people shall be delivered, every one who is found written in the book. And many of those who sleep in the dust of the earth shall awake, some to everlasting life, some to shame *and* everlasting contempt. Those who are wise shall shine like the brightness of the firmament, and those who turn many to righteousness like the stars forever and ever. (Daniel 12:1–3 NKJV)

For the grace of God that brings salvation has appeared to all men, teaching us that, denying ungodliness and worldly lusts, we should live soberly, righteously, and godly in the present age, looking for the blessed hope and glorious appearing of our great God and Savior Jesus Christ, who gave Himself for us, that He might redeem us from every lawless deed and purify for Himself His own special people, zealous for good works. (Titus 2:11–14 NKJV)

In the late 1800s, Thomas O. Chisolm and William

J. Kirkpatrick combined their talents to pen the words and music of the song "O to Be Like Thee." It was the timeless hearts' cry of those two men and should be that of the church today:

> O to be like Thee! blessèd Redeemer,
>
> This is my constant longing and prayer;
>
> Gladly I'll forfeit all of earth's treasures,
>
> Jesus, Thy perfect likeness to wear.
>
> O to be like Thee! Full of compassion,
>
> Loving, forgiving, tender and kind,
>
> Helping the helpless, cheering the fainting,
>
> Seeking the wandering sinner to find.
>
> Refrain:
>
> O to be like Thee! O to be like Thee,
>
> Blessèd Redeemer, pure as Thou art;
>
> Come in Thy sweetness, come in Thy fullness;
>
> Stamp Thine own image deep on my heart.[189]

ENDNOTES

1. Lance Pape, Brite Divinity School, Texas Christian University, Fort Worth, TX, http://www.workingpreacher.org/preaching.aspx?commentary_id=2201; accessed June 2016.

2. "The Book of Acts," http://www.bible-history.com/new-testament/bookofacts.html; accessed May 2016.

3. Richard Longenecker, *The Expositor's Bible Commentary* (Grand Rapids, MI: Zondervan, 1995), 207.

4. "Alexander MacLaren's Exposition of Holy Scripture, Acts 1," http://www.studylight.org/commentaries/mac/acts-1.html; accessed May 2016.

5. John Stott, *The Message of Acts (Bible Speaks Today)* (Downer's Grove, IL: InterVarsity Press, 1990), 69.

6. http://midwaypca.org/messenger_pdf/June%202009.pdf; accessed May 2016.

7. Revelation 17:14

8. Eusebius, *The History of the Church* (translated by G.A. Williamson) (London, England: Penguin Books, 1965), 65.

9. Public Domain.

10. John Pollock, *The Apostle: A Life of Paul* (Colorado Springs, CO: Cook Communications Ministries, 1985), 18–19.

11. http://bibleapps.com/commentaries/acts/9-2.htm; accessed June 2016.

12. "Calvin's Commentary on the Bible, Acts 9," https://www.studylight.org/commentaries/cal/acts-9.html; accessed May 2016.

13. Charles Swindoll, *Paul: A Man of Grace and Grit* (Nashville, TN: W Publishing Group, 2002), 27.

14. Richard C. H. Lenski, *The Interpretation of St. Paul's First and Second Epistle to the Corinthians* (Columbus, OH: Wartburg Press, 1937; later edition by Augsberg Fortress, Minneapolis, MN: 1963), 1287–1288.

15. Bill Combs, "Did Saul Change His Name to Paul?" June 10, 2012, http://www.dbts.edu/2012/06/10/did-saul-change-his-name-to-paul/; accessed May 2016.

16. "Observations on the Conversion and Apostleship of St. Paul" by Lord Lyttelton, Analyzed and Condensed by Rev. J. L. Campbell, D. D., Cambridge, Massachusetts, http://grandoldbook.com/convofsaullytt.pdf; accessed May 2016.

17. Jewish Virtual Library, "Agrippa I," http://www.jewishvirtuallibrary.org/jsource/judaica/ejud_0002_0001_0_00542.html; accessed August 2015.

18. Michael Farquhar, *A Treasury of Royal Scandals* (New York: Penguin Books, 2001), 209.

19. Flavius Josephus, *Antiquities*, 15, 403 ff. http://www.templemount.org/destruct2.html#anchor596423; accessed August 2015.

20. http://legal-dictionary.thefreedictionary.com/eminent+domain; accessed July 2016.

21. John Pollock, *The Apostle: A Life of Paul* (Colorado Springs, CO: David C. Cook, 2012), 296–297

22. Cornelius Tacitus, *The Annals,* Book 15, Chapter 44, Alfred John Church, William Jackson Brodribb, Ed. http://www.perseus.tufts.edu/hopper/text?doc=Perseus%3Atext%3A1999.02.0078%3Abook%3D15%3Achapter%3D44; accessed May 2016.

23. Rev. Gaylin R. Schmeling, "Two Thousand Years of Grace," http://www.blts.edu/wp-content/uploads/2011/06/GRS-2000.pdf; accessed May 2016.

24. Ray C. Stedman, *What's This World Coming To?* (An expository study of Matthew 24–26, the Olivet Discourse), (Palo Alto, CA: Discovery Publications, 1970), http://www.templemount.org/destruct2.html#anchor615789; accessed August 2015.

25. The Apology of Tertullian, tr. and annotated by W. Reeve; and the Meditations of the emperor Marcus Aurelius Antoninus, tr. by J. Collier. xvi. 270. [1889.] Series: Ancient and modern library of theological literature 31. (Details from Bodleian online catalogue.) Tertullian portion only contained here: http://www.tertullian.org/articles/reeve_apology.htm; accessed May 2016.

26. "Polycarp-Martyrdom," http://www.polycarp.net/; accessed May 2016.

27. John Carlin, "Christian Persecutions in the First Three Centuries," http://www.theologytable.com/new%20documents/Persecutions%5B1%5D.pdf; accessed May 2016.

28. Mark Galli, "Persecution in the Early Church: A Gallery of the Persecuting Emperors," https://www.christianhistoryinstitute.org/magazine/article/persecution-in-early-church-gallery/; accessed May 2016.

29. "When Was the Book of Revelation Written?" https://readingacts.com/2016/04/05/when-was-the-book-of-revelation-written/; accessed May 2016.

30. Mark Galli, "Persecution in the Early Church: A Gallery of the Persecuting Emperors," https://www.christianhistoryinstitute.org/magazine/article/persecution-in-early-church-gallery/; accessed May 2016.

31. J. Lebreton, "St. Justin Martyr," *The Catholic Encyclopedia* (New York: Robert Appleton Company, 1910); accessed May 2016.

32. Eusebius, 180.

33. Dan Graves, MSL, "Fabian, the 1st Martyr under Decius," http://www. christianity.com/church/church-history/timeline/1-300/fabian-the-1st-martyr-under-decius-11629620.html; accessed May 2016.

34. John Chapman, "St. Cyprian of Carthage," *The Catholic Encyclopedia*. Vol. 4, (New York: Robert Appleton Company, 1908,), http://www.newadvent.org/ cathen/04583b.htm; accessed May 2016.

35. Michael Grant, *The Roman Emperors: A Biographical Guide to the Rulers of Imperial Rome, 31 B.C. – A.D. 476* (reprint edition, Barnes &Noble, 1997), 165.

36. James Carroll, *Constantine's Sword: The Church and the Jews, A History* (Boston, MA, New York, NY: Houghton Mifflin Co. 2002), 170

37. Lactantius, *De Mortibus Persecutorum* 44.4–6, translated by J. L. Creed, *Lactantius: De Mortibus Persecutorum* (Oxford: Oxford University Press, 1984), quoted by Noel Lenski in *The Cambridge Companion to the Age of Constantine, Vol. 13*, 71.

38. "Galerius and Constantine: Edicts of Toleration 311/313," Fordham University, http://legacy.fordham.edu/Halsall/source/edict-milan.asp; accessed May 2016.

39. J. Stevenson (Editor), W. H. C. Frend (Editor), *A New Eusebius: Documents Illustrating the History of the Church to AD 337* (Grand Rapids, MI: Baker Academic, A division of Baker Publishing Group, 2013), 383.

40. Simon Sebag Montefiore, *Jerusalem: The Biography* (London, England: Weidenfeld & Nicolson, an imprint of The Orion Publishing Group, 2011), 145.

41. Nicene Creed, AD 325, *Christian Apologetics and Research Ministry,* 2013, from www.carm.org/what-trinity; accessed June 2016.

42. Eusebius, *The History of the Church*, Introduction, xii

43. Pastor Carolyn Dipboye, "Bearing the Cross: communion meditation," March 13, 2011, http://www.gracecovenantoakridge.net/images/11-03-13.ser.pdf; accessed May 2016.

44. Greg Laurie, "What the Cross Means," 5.20.2010, https://www.harvest.org/ devotions-and-blogs/daily-devotions/2010-05-20; accessed June 2016.

45. A. R. Birley, "St Helena, Discoverer of the True Cross (250–330)" http://www. brown.edu/Research/Breaking_Ground/bios/St.%20Helena_Flavia%20 Julia%20Helena%20Augusta.pdf

46. "Constantine the Great and His Personal Tragedies," http://neobyzantium. com/constantine-the-great-and-his-personal-tragedies/; accessed June 2016.

47. FR. William Saunders, "St. Helena and the True Cross," http://www. catholiceducation.org/en/culture/catholic-contributions/st-helena-and-the-true-cross.html; accessed June 2016.

48. A. R. Birley, "St. Helena, Discoverer of the True Cross (250–330)"

49. Philip Schaff, *History of the Christian Church: Vol. II: From Constantine the Great to Gregory the Great A.D. 311–600* (New York: Charles Scribner, 1867), 380.

50. Carroll, 183.

51. S. Michael Houdmann, "Was St. Peter the First Pope?" Got Questions Ministries, http://www.gotquestions.org/Peter-first-pope.html; accessed March 2016.

52. John Cornwell, *Hitler's Pope: The Secret History of Pius XII* (New York, NY: Penguin Group, 2008), 25.

53. Megan McArdle, "Happy Easter, Which is Not Named After Ishtar, Okay?" 3.29.13, http://www.thedailybeast.com/articles/2013/03/29/happy-easter-which-is-not-named-after-ishtar-okay.html; accessed June 2016.

54. William Smith, LLD, William Wayte, G. E. Marindin, Ed, *A Dictionary of Greek and Roman Antiquities* (1890), Saturna'lia, http://www.perseus.tufts.edu/hopper/text?doc=Perseus:text:1999.04.0063:entry=saturnalia-cn; accessed June 2016,

55. Adam Clarke Commentary, Matthew 2, http://www.studylight.org/commentaries/acc/matthew-2.html; accessed June 2016.

56. Dr. David R. Reagan, "When Was Jesus Born?" http://christinprophecy.org/articles/when-was-jesus-born/; accessed June 2016.

57. Rev. J. D. Shaw, "This Do In Remembrance of Me," May 11, 2014, Grace Bible Church, http://www.gracebibleofoxford.com/resources/sermons/this-do-in-remembrance-of-me/; accessed June 2016.

58. http://www.oxfordbiblicalstudies.com/article/opr/t94/e602; accessed June 2016.

59. "Constantine the Great," http://www.catholic.com/encyclopedia/constantine-the-great; accessed June 2016.

60. Peter Nathan, "Orthodoxy: Just Another Heresy?" Fall, 2005, Vision.org, https://vision.org/visionmedia/article.aspx%3Fid%3D145; accessed June 2016.

61. Jack Wellman, "Does Baptism Save You: A Biblical Analysis," http://www.whatchristianswanttoknow.com/does-baptism-save-you-a-biblical-analysis/#ixzz4CPdT0wlR; accessed June 2016.

62. Montifiore, 149.

63. Raul Hillberg, *The Destruction of the European Jews* (New York, NY: Holmes and Meier, 1985), 7f.

64. Fr. Juan Velez, "Chrysostom's Spiritual Renewal - Cardinal Newman," http://www.cardinaljohnhenrynewman.com/chrysostoms-spiritual-renewal-cardinal-newman/; accessed June 2016.

65. James Parkes, *The Conflict of the Church and the Synagogue: A Study in the Origins of Antisemitism,* (New York: JPS, 1934); http://legacy.fordham.edu/halsall/source/chrysostom-jews6.asp; accessed June 2016.

66. Dennis Prager and Joseph Telushkin, *Why the Jews? The Reason for Antisemitism* (New York, NY: Touchstone, an imprint of Simon Schuster, Inc., 2016), 78.

67. "St. John Chrysostom's On the Jews," (III, article 1), http://www.catholicapologetics.info/apologetics/judaism/jchrsos.htm#I; accessed June 2016.

68. "William Tyndale," http://greatsite.com/timeline-english-bible-history/william-tyndale.html; accessed June 2016.

69. Bernard Starr, "'Christ Killers': The Hidden Agenda," *Huffington Post*, August 20, 2013, http://www.huffingtonpost.com/bernard-starr/christ-killers-the-hidden_b_3463252.html; accessed June 2016.

70. Ibid.

71. Peter Heather, *The Fall of the Roman Empire: A New History of Rome and the Barbarians* (Oxford, England: Oxford University Press, 2007), 191.

72. Professor H. Graetz, *History of the Jews*, Vol. III, Philadelphia: The Jewish Publication Society of America, 45.

73. Solomon Katz, *Monographs of the Mediaeval Academy of America No. 12: The Jews in the Visigothic and Frankish Kingdoms of Spain and Gaul* (Cambridge, Massachusetts: The Mediaeval Society of America, 1937), 10.

74. Yom Tov Assis, *The Jews of Spain: From Settlement to Expulsion* (Jerusalem: The Hebrew University of Jerusalem, 1988), 10.

75. Katz, 13.

76. Ibid., 16.

77. Ibid., 21.

78. "Seventeenth Council of Toledo," http://en.wikipedia.org/wiki/Seventeenth_Council_of_Toledo; accessed April 2014.

79. Norman Roth (1994), *Jews, Visigoths and Muslims in Medieval Spain: Cooperation and Conflict* (Leiden: Brill, 1994), 79–90.

80. Norman Stillman, "Aspects of Jewish Life in Islamic Spain" in *Aspects of Jewish Culture in the Middle Ages*, ed. Paul E. Szarmach (Albany: State University of New York Press, 1979), 53.

81. Benzion Netanyahu, *The Origins of the Inquisition in Fifteenth Century Spain* (New York: Random House, 1995), 54.

82. Carroll, 324.

83. "The Treatment of Jews," https://www.jewishvirtuallibrary.org/jsource/anti-semitism/Jews_in_Arab_lands_(gen).html; accessed June 2016.

84. Deanna Proach, "Emich of Lusingen Attacks the Jews," http://www.crusadesandcrusaders.com/2013/01/06/the-demise-of-the-rhineland-jews/; accessed June 2016.

85. Montefiore, 207–210.

86. Ibid, 212.

87. Thomas F. Madden, "The Real History of the Crusades," http://www.catholicculture.org/culture/library/view.cfm?recnum=4461; accessed July 2016.

88. Edward Flannery, *The Anguish of the Jews: Twenty-three Centuries of Antisemitism* (Mahwah, NJ: Paulist Press, 1985), 91–92.

89. Marc Saperstein, *Moments of Crisis in Jewish-Christian Relations* (Philadelphia, PA: Trinity Press International, 1989), 20.

90. Roger of Howden, *Gesta Regis Ricardi* (Trans. Henry Riley), https://www.jewishvirtuallibrary.org/jsource/History/hoveden.html; accessed July 2016.

91. http://www.historyofyork.org.uk/themes/norman/the-1190-massacre; accessed July 2016.

92. Heinz Schreckenburg, *The Jews in Christian Art* (New York, NY: Continuum, 1996), 15.

93. http://www.shalomadventure.com/jewish-life/cooking-2/1448-calendar-of-jewish-persecution; accessed July 2016.

94. A religious or moral act that causes others to reverence God; *esp* : religious martyrdom in times of persecution; http://www.merriam-webster.com/dictionary/kiddush%20hashem; accessed April 2014.

95. Nissan Mindel, "The Massacre of 5151," http://www.chabad.org/library/article_cdo/aid/112389/jewish/The-Massacres-of-5151.htm; accessed April 2014.

96. Netanyahu, 135–136.

97. A historically controversial area of Western Europe lying in western Germany along both banks of the middle Rhine River.

98. The Jews were often accused of causing the Plague to destroy Christiansf, even though Jews and Muslims were as likely to be infected as Christians. After being tortured, some Jews confessed that they were poisoning wells and other water sources, creating the Plague. As a result, Jews were expelled or killed by the thousands. As a result of forced confessions, the entire Jewish population of Strassburg, Germany, was given the choice to convert to Christianity or be burned on rows of stakes on a platform in the city's burial ground. About 2,000 were killed. http://facts.randomhistory.com/2009/06/09_black-death.html; accessed May 2014.

99. Helen Rawlings, *The Spanish Inquisition* (Hoboken, NJ: Wiley-Blackwell, 2005), 53.

100. At their annual party rally, the Nazis announce new laws that revoke Reich citizenship for Jews and prohibit Jews from marrying or having sexual relations with persons of "German or related blood." "Racial infamy," as this becomes known, is made a criminal offense. The Nuremberg Laws define a "Jew" as someone with three or four Jewish grandparents. Consequently, the Nazis classify as Jews thousands of people who had converted from Judaism to another religion, among them even Roman Catholic priests and nuns and Protestant ministers whose grandparents were Jewish; http://www.ushmm.org/outreach/en/article.php?ModuleId=10007695; accessed May 2014.

101. Netanyahu, 351.

102. Antonio Martin Gamero, *Historía de la ciudad de Toledo* (University of Michigan, 2007), 1038. http://books.google.com/books/about/Historía_de_la_ciudad_de_Toledo.html?id=0JpNAAAAMAAJ; accessed May 2014.

103. Benzion Netanyahu, *Don Isaac Abravanel: Statesman & Philosopher* (Ithaca, NY: Cornell University Press: 1953), 42–43.

104. Ibid., 43.

105. "History of Anti-Semitism," http://southerninstitute.info/holocaust_education/ds1.html; accessed May 2014.

106. Andres Bernaldez, *Memorias del reinadode los Reyes Catolicos*, ed. Manuel Gomez-Moreno y Juan de M. Carriazo, 1962; 920. Translated by Benzion Netanyahu in *The Origins of the Inquisition in Fifteenth Century Spain*, 1053.

107. "Deathly Silence," http://southerninstitute.info/holocaust_education/ds1.html; accessed May 2014.

108. *The Free Dictionary*, http://www.thefreedictionary.com/Burghers; accessed April 2014.

109. Netanyahu, *Don Isaac Abravanel: Statesman & Philosopher*, 45.

110. Netanyahu, *The Origins of the Inquisition in Fifteenth Century Spain*, xiv.

111. "Thomás de Torquemada and the Spanish Inquisition," http://bit.ly/2fsDUao accessed May 2014.

112. G. CH. Lee, *The History of the Inquisition in the Middle Ages*, "Brokgauz-Efron," Saint Petersburg, 1914 *(in Russian)* as stated on http://godspeakstoday.info/sh_biblio.html#r56; accessed April 2014.

113. Augustine, *Expositions on the Book of Psalms*, IV, Library of Fathers, Vol. 32, Veritatis Splendor Publications 2012, Amazon Digital Services, 79.2.

114. Dagobert D. Runes, *The War Against the Jews* (New York, NY: Philosophical Library, Inc., 2008), 18.

115. Inquisition, *Jewish Encyclopedia*, http://jewishencyclopedia.com/articles/8122-inquisition; accessed April 2014.

116. Jane S. Gerber, *The Jews of Spain* (New York: The Free Press, 1994), 127. (See A. Sicroff, Les Controverses des statuts de puerte de sang en Espagna du XVe au Xviie siècle (Paris, 1960).

117. "Tomás de Torquemada," http://bit.ly/2fsDUao; accessed April 2016.

118. Luna was constable of Castile, ruler of Castile during much of the reign of the weak John II. He was the illegitimate son of a noble of Aragonese descent and the only distinguished statesman during a dismal period in Castilian history. For many years his main efforts were concerned with saving the crown from armed factions of dissident magnates who sought to control it. http://www.britannica.com/EBchecked/topic/351334/Alvaro-de-Luna; accessed May 2014.

119. Netanyahu, *The Origins of the Inquisition in Fifteenth Century Spain*, 500.

120. Nicholas of Lyra, *Postillae perpetuae in universam S. Scripturam* (Commentary Notes to the Universal Holy Scripture). From 1319 he headed the Franciscans in France and in 1325 founded the College of Burgundy from where he wrote a 50-volume exegesis on the Scriptures; Volume on Deuteronomy, 335.

121. The Phoenician wife of Ahab who according to the account in I and II Kings pressed the cult of Baal on the Israelite kingdom but was finally killed in accordance with Elijah's prophecy, http://www.merriam-webster.com/dictionary/jezebel; accessed April 2014.

122. Cecil Roth, *The Spanish Inquisition* (New York: W.W. Norton & Co, 1964), 267.

123. William Jones, *The History of the Christian Church* (Great Britain: Ages Software, 1997), 88.

124. "Torquemada's Spanish Inquisition: From Suspicion to Death," http://deni-edwards.hubpages.com/hub/Torquemadas-Spanish-Inquisition-From-Suspicion-to-Death; accessed May 2014.

125. Miroslav Hroch & Anna Skybova, *Ecclesia Militans: The Inquisition* (New York: Dorset Press, 1988), 145.

126. http://www.catholicpeacefellowship.org/nextpage.asp?m=2272; accessed April 2014.

127. Hroch & Skybova, 146.

128. "Torture Techniques of the Spanish Inquisition," http://jamesray.hubpages.com/hub/Killing-in-the-Name-of-God; accessed April 2014.

129. Thomas Cahill, *Heretics and Heroes: How Renaissance Artists and Reformation Priests Created our World* (New York: Doubleday, a division of Randon House, 2013), 49–50.

130. Netanyahu, *The Origins of the Inquisition in Fifteenth Century Spain,* 132.

131. One of the most famous victims of the Inquisition was Joan of Arc of France who, following the Battle of Orleans, was tried by the French for sorcery and heresy and was burned at the stake in 1431 at the age of 19.

132. Psalm 107:23.

133. Salvador de Madariaga, *Christopher Columbus: Being the Life of the Very Magnificent Lord Don Christobal Colon* (New York: McMillan, 1940), 168.

134. Elijah Capsali, *Seder Eliyahu Zuta* ed. A. Shmuelevitz (Tel Aviv University: Jerusalem, 1975), chapter 69.

135. Samuel Eliot Morison, *Admiral of the Ocean Sea: A Life of Christopher Columbus* (New York: Little Brown and Company, 1942, renewed 1970), 105.

136. Baer, *A History of the Jews in Christian Spain* (Philadelphia: The Jewish Publication Society, 1993), 421.

137. Capsali, chapter 67 as quoted in *The Jews of Spain: A History of the Sephardic Experience* (Jane S. Gerber: New York: The Free Press, 1992), 136.

138. Leo W. Schwarz, ed., *Memoirs of My People* (New York: Jewish Publication Society of America, 1945), 46–47.

139. Simon Wiesenthal, *Sails of Hope: The Secret Mission of Christopher Columbus* (translated from German by Richard and Clara Winston); (New York: Macmillan Publishing Co., Inc., 1973), 54.

140. "The Diary of Luis De Torres," *Los Angeles Jewish Times*, December 24, 1999.

141. Samuel Usque, *Consolation for the Tribulations of Israel,* edited and translated by Martin A. Cohen (Philadelphia: Jewish Publication Society, 1965), 201–202.

142. Benzion Netanyahu, *Don Isaac Abravanel: Statesman & Philosopher* (Ithaca, NY: Cornell University Press: 1953), 57–58.

143. Netanyahu, *Don Isaac Abravanel: Statesman & Philosopher,* 63.

144. Ibid., 64.

145. Eric W. Gritsch, *Martin Luther's Anti-Semitism: Against His Better Judgment* (Grand Rapids, MI: William B. Eerdmans Publishing Company, 2012), 26–27.

146. Texts from the History of the Relationship, Martin Luther, "That Jesus Was Born A Jew," (1523), Excerpts, http://ccjr.us/dialogika-resources/primary-texts-from-the-history-of-the-relationship/272-luther-1523; accessed July 2016.

147. "German Peasant Rebellion 1525," http://www.revolutionprotestencyclopedia.com/fragr_image/media/IEO_German_Peasant_Rebellion; accessed July 2016.

148. Saperstein, *Moments of Crisis*, 29.

149. "Martin Luther, "The Jews and Their Lies," http://www. jewishvirtuallibrary.org/jsource/anti-semitism/Luther_on_Jews.html; accessed July 2016.

150. Daphne M. Olsen, "Luther and Hitler: A Linear Connection between Martin Luther and Adolf Hitler's Anti-Semitism with a Nationalistic Foundation," http://scholarship.rollins.edu/cgi/viewcontent. cgi?article=1019&context=mls; accessed July 2016. (Citation: William Nicholls, *Christian Antisemitism: A History of Hate* (New Jersey: Jason Aronson Inc., 1993)

151. Peter F. Wiener, Martin Luther, Hitler's Spiritual Ancestor (New York, NY: Hutchinson & Co. Publishers), http://www.catholicapologetics.info/ apologetics/protestantism/spancestor.htm#character; accessed July 2016.

152. *babylon.com*, Free Online Dictionary; http://www.babylon.com/definition/ Supercession/English; accessed June 2010.

153. Michael D. Evans, *The American Prophecies: Ancient Scriptures Reveal our Nation's Future* (New York, NY: Warner Faith, 2004), 55–56.

154. "Here and There," *Pentecostal Evangel*, August 18, 1923, 8.

155. Quoted by Carroll, *Constantine's Sword*, 376.

156. https://en.wikipedia.org/wiki/Pogrom; accessed July 2016.

157. Robert Weinberg, "The Pogrom of 1905 in Odessa: A Case Study" in *Pogroms: Anti-Jewish Violence in Modern Russian History*, John D. Klier and Shlomo Lambroza, eds. (Cambridge, 1992), http://faculty.history.umd.edu/ BCooperman/NewCity/Pogrom1905.html; accessed July 2016.

158. Joseph Alexander Norland, "In Memoriam: Col. Richard Meinertzhagen," *The Israel Report*, June 17, 2004; http://www.cdn-friends-icej.ca/isreport/ mayjun04/meinertzhagen.html; accessed August 2011.

159. Hannah Weiner and Sheba E. Sweet, *Blood and Fury, A Historical Memoir of the 1919 Pogroms in the Ukraine* (Amazon.com Kindle version, 1986 & 2013), "The First Victims," https://www.amazon.com/Blood-Fury-Historical-Pogroms-Ukraine-ebook/dp/B01B109KBC/ref=sr_1_1?s=digital-text&ie=UTF8&qid=1469118234&sr=1-1#reader_B01B109KBC; accessed July 2016.

160. Klaus Scholder, *Die Kirchen und das Dritte Reich*, vol. 1, *Borgeschichte und Zeit der Illusionen 1918–1934* (Frankfurt am Main, 1977), pp. 338ff, in Saul Friedlander, *Nazi Germany and the Jews, Volume 1: The Years of Persecution, 1933–1939* (New York: Harper Collins Publishers, 1997), 42.

161. Thomas Mann, *The Letters of Thomas Mann 1889–1955* (London, 1985), 170.

162. *Microsoft® Encarta® Encyclopedia 2000*. (Redmond Washington: Microsoft Corporation, 1993–1999), s.v., "Hitler, Adolf."

163. Pavel Friedman, "I Never Saw Another Butterfly," http://voiceseducation. org/node/561; accessed July 2016.

164. *Microsoft® Encarta® Encyclopedia 2000.*, s.v., "Holocaust."

165. Geoffrey G. Field, *Evangelist of Race: The Germanic Vision of Houston Stewart Chamberlain* (New York: Columbia University Press, 1981), 90.

166. Robert Solomon Wistrich, *Who's Who in Nazi Germany* (Hove, East Sussex, UK: Psychology Press, 2002), 118.

167. John Toland, *Adolf Hitler* (London: Book Club Associates, 1977), 116.

168. Houston Stewart Chamberlain, *Letters* (1882–1924 and correspondence with Emperor Wilhelm II), (Munich: F. Bruckmann, 1928), 124. (Translated from the German by Alexander Jacob.)

169. "Adolf Hitler," *Deutsche Presse*, April 20–21, 1944, 1.

170. Ibid.

171. "Germany Must be Told," *Christian Century*, 50 (August 4, 1933), 1033.

172. "Anti-Semitism," RR, 3 (Summer 1938), 5.

173. See William G. Chrystal, *Young Reinhold Niebuhr: His Early Writings, 1911–1931*, (St. Louis, MO, 1977), 17.

174. "The Catholic Heresy," *Christian Century*, 54 (December 6, 1937), 324.

175. Deborah E. Lipstadt, *Beyond Belief: The American Press and the Coming of the Holocaust, 1933–1945* (New York: Simon and Schuster, 1993), 79–80.

176. "Wannsee Conference, *Jewish Virtual Library*; http://www. jewishvirtuallibrary.org/jsource/judaica/ejud_0002_0020_0_20606.html; accessed March 2012.

177. Felix Frankfurter, "Selective Outrage on Campus," *The Jerusalem Post*, July 22, 2016, http://www.jpost.com/Opinion/Selective-outrage-on-campus-432930; accessed July 2016.

178. Helene Cooper and Steven Lee Myers, "Palestinians Pursue U.N. Seat," *New York Times*, September 22, 2011; accessed September 2011.

179. "The Abrahamic Blessing," *Pentecostal Evangel*, July 29, 1933, 7.

180. Hermann Rauschning, *Gesprache mit Hitler* (Zurich: Europa Verlag, 1959), op. 210–211; cf. *The Voice of Destruction* (New York: Putnam, 1940), 223–224.

181. Msgr. John Oesterreicher, "Auschwitz, the Christian, and the Council," *CatholicCulture.org*;

182. "Latest Trends in Religious Restrictions and Hostilities," Pew Research Center, February 26, 2015, http://www.pewforum.org/2015/02/26/religious-hostilities/; accessed July 2016.

183. Mark Frauenfelder, "Congressman Hank Johnson says his description of Jewish settlers as "termites" was a "poor choice of words," http://boingboing.net/2016/07/26/congressman-hank-johnson-says.html, July 26, 2016; accessed July 2016.

184. Katrina Lantos Swett, M. Zuhdi Jasser and Hannah Rosenthal, "An Unsafe Place for Jews," *U.S. News and World Report*, April 2, 2015, http://www.uscirf.gov/news-room/op-eds/us-news-and-world-report-unsafe-place-jews; accessed July 2016.

185. http://www.brainyquote.com/quotes/topics/topic_history.html; accessed July 2016.

186. C. H. Spurgeon, "Building the Church," April 5, 1874, http://www.biblebb.com/files/spurgeon/1167.htm; accessed July 2016.

187. http://www.religionfacts.com/christianity/branches; accessed July 2016.

188. Chris Armstrong, *Contemporary Church Early Ressourcement*, Kindle Version, https://www.amazon.co.uk/Contemporary-Church-Early-Ressourcement-Evangelical/dp/1606088998/254-1872209-7518132?ie=UTF8&*Version*=1&*entries*=0#reader_B014I5DDGU; accessed July 2016.

189. http://www.cyberhymnal.org/htm/o/t/o2belike.htm; accessed July 2016.

MICHAEL DAVID EVANS, the #1 *New York Times* bestselling author, is an award-winning journalist/Middle East analyst. Dr. Evans has appeared on hundreds of network television and radio shows including *Good Morning America, Crossfire* and *Nightline*, and *The Rush Limbaugh Show*, and on Fox Network, *CNN World News*, NBC, ABC, and CBS. His articles have been published in the *Wall Street Journal, USA Today, Washington Times, Jerusalem Post* and newspapers worldwide. More than twenty-five million copies of his books are in print, and he is the award-winning producer of nine documentaries based on his books.

Dr. Evans is considered one of the world's leading experts on Israel and the Middle East, and is one of the most sought-after speakers on that subject. He is the chairman of the board of the ten Boom Holocaust Museum in Haarlem, Holland, and is the founder of Israel's first Christian museum located in the Friends of Zion Heritage Center in Jerusalem.

Dr. Evans has authored a number of books including: *History of Christian Zionism, Showdown with Nuclear Iran, Atomic Iran, The Next Move Beyond Iraq, The Final Move Beyond Iraq*, and *Countdown*. His body of work also includes the novels *Seven Days, GameChanger, The Samson Option, The Four Horsemen, The Locket, Born Again: 1967*, and *The Columbus Code*.

✦ ✦ ✦

Michael David Evans is available to speak or for interviews.
Contact: EVENTS@drmichaeldevans.com.

BOOKS BY: MIKE EVANS

Israel: America's Key to Survival

Save Jerusalem

The Return

Jerusalem D.C.

Purity and Peace of Mind

Who Cries for the Hurting?

Living Fear Free

I Shall Not Want

Let My People Go

Jerusalem Betrayed

Seven Years of Shaking: A Vision

The Nuclear Bomb of Islam

Jerusalem Prophecies

Pray For Peace of Jerusalem

America's War:
The Beginning of the End

The Jerusalem Scroll

The Prayer of David

The Unanswered Prayers of Jesus

God Wrestling

The American Prophecies

Beyond Iraq: The Next Move

The Final Move beyond Iraq

Showdown with Nuclear Iran

Jimmy Carter: The Liberal Left
and World Chaos

Atomic Iran

Cursed

Betrayed

The Light

Corrie's Reflections & Meditations

The Revolution

The Final Generation

Seven Days

The Locket

Persia: The Final Jihad

GAMECHANGER SERIES:

GameChanger

Samson Option

The Four Horsemen

THE PROTOCOLS SERIES:

The Protocols

The Candidate

Jerusalem

The History of Christian Zionism

Countdown

Ten Boom: Betsie, Promise of God

Commanded Blessing

Born Again: 1948

Born Again: 1967

Presidents in Prophecy

Stand with Israel

Prayer, Power and Purpose

Turning Your Pain Into Gain

Christopher Columbus, Secret Jew

Living in the F.O.G.

Finding Favor with God

Finding Favor with Man

Unleashing God's Favor

The Jewish State: The Volunteers

See You in New York

Friends of Zion: Patterson & Wingate

The Columbus Code

The Temple

Satan, You Can't Have My Country!

Satan, You Can't Have Israel!

Lights in the Darkness

The Seven Feasts of Israel

Netanyahu

Jew-Hatred and the Church

COMING SOON:

The Visionaries

TO PURCHASE, CONTACT: orders@timeworthybooks.
com P. O. BOX 30000, PHOENIX, AZ 85046